What people are saying abou

Have you ever had a moment when you wondered, "God, where are You?" I think we've all been there. Jeff Leake has written a book that honestly examines his own struggles with an understanding that God sometimes seems distant and inactive. If you're in the middle of a storm in life, *God in Motion* will reassure you that God is working, even when you cannot see Him. Check out Jeff's book. I know you'll be encouraged!

— Greg Surratt, Lead Pastor at Seacoast Church,
   Charleston, South Carolina
   Author of *Ir-Rev-Rend*

If you've ever felt like God was distant, disconnected or silent, don't worry—you're not alone. Oh, Jeff Leake gets it! In *God in Motion,* Jeff makes practical what you may have always thought was theoretical—how to hear from God when you think He's not saying anything at all! You've got to read this book.

— Matt Keller, Lead Pastor at Next Level Church,
   Fort Myers, Florida
   Author of *The God of the Underdogs,* MattKellerOnline.com

Jeff Leake's grasp of spiritual realities is both thrilling and challenging. In his book, *God in Motion,* he explains that despair is often rooted in the misconception that God is inactive, unaware, and indifferent. With powerful teaching and heartwarming stories, Jeff assures us God is active—He's already in motion—even when we can't detect His hand at work.

— George O. Wood, General Superintendent
   Assemblies of God, USA, Springfield, Missouri

Every time I listen to my friend, Jeff, I learn something that impacts my journey with Jesus. What an insightful leader and teacher! I love Jeff's depiction of Jesus. *God in Motion* is authentic, applicable, and immediately practical. People who read this book will walk away encouraged and growing. Read it and recommend it to those you want to encourage in their journey.

— Ron Heitman, Senior Pastor at Evangel Church,
    Chicago, Illinois

Speaking out of his practical pastoral experience and his own extensive journey of faith, Pastor Jeff Leake wrestles in this book with the kinds of real life issues we all face every day. And, rather than varnish them with simplistic solutions, he uses solid biblical theology to build his view of God and how God works in our lives. I will definitely include this book on my list of gifts to give to my friends who need to be encouraged, enlightened, inspired, and challenged.

— Dr. Don Meyer, President of Valley Forge Christian College,
    Schuylkill, Pennsylvania

For those of us who sometimes think that God is inactive, unaware, or indifferent, this book is a powerful reminder that God is always in motion— preparing a hope-filled future for us. Jeff is a life-long student of God's Word and an astute observer of human experience. In this book, he skillfully weaves together poignant stories and time-tested biblical principles to show us that God is always working on our behalf as we patiently and persistently pursue His heart and purpose.

— John Palmer, President of Emerge Ministries,
    Akron, Ohio

My dear friend, Pastor Jeff Leake of Pittsburgh, teaches you how you can enter into God's multiplication, His adventures, and His wonderful rest. It is obvious that God is in motion in the MCM Network, led by Pastor Jeff, by the speed he plants churches all over America and beyond! The leading of the Holy Spirit brings ultimate ripple effects beyond our wildest imaginations because our God is a God in motion.

— Johannes Amritzer, President of Evangelical Mission SOS International,
    Stockholm, Sweden

God in Motion is a compelling guide for both the seasoned believer and those who are young in their faith. Jeff Leake writes clearly and personally about how God is working, no matter what our natural eyes can see. Through personal anecdotes, biblical examples, and thought-provoking questions, he engages us in super-natural awareness of God's constant activity. He considers the challenges readers may face in living this out, yet compels them to embrace the truth that God is both interested in and investing into their lives. Jeff isn't just putting some good ideas into writing; he is living them out by successfully reaching people, making disciples, and multiplying leaders.

— Rev. Brian Bolt, Founder of the CityReach Network,
  Pittsburgh, Pennsylvania

Jeff Leake is a leader whom God has set into motion for this crucial point in history. As an effective pastor, Jeff shares insights from his life and ministry experiences that will elevate your faith and keep you focused on the fact that God is at work in you and through you!

— Doug Clay, Treasurer, Assemblies of God, USA,
  Springfield, Missouri

Have you ever had a moment when you felt God had bailed out on you . . . that He just closed the door and walked out of your life? Then this book is for you! Like an artist laying oils on a canvas in a beautiful, self-effacing style, Pastor Jeff Leake composes a portrait revealing a God so big that He can do anything, yet so personal that He cares about everything. This book will stir your heart and fire up your faith as you realize that even when you don't see him, God is as close as your breath! He really is at work in your life!

— Ron Johnson, Lead Pastor of One Church,
  Orlando, Florida

Jeff Leake's unique ability to align himself with the heart of God has inspired me for more than ten years. I'm in Philadelphia today leading a new church because Jeff sensed God's activity here before it became obvious to me. Through Jeff's life, I've been impacted by the principles articulated in this book. That's why I eagerly read it, knowing that every insight has been field-tested in the trenches of his personal life and ministry. I hope you'll read it and discover what God has been up to in the background of your life.

— Brad Leach, Lead Pastor at CityLife Church,
   South Philadelphia, Pennsylvania

Every time I'm with Jeff Leake, I come away feeling like I know this "God in motion" just a little better. Encouragement, acceptance, forgiveness, and a deep kindness come through every breath and every word. As I studied these principles and saw Jeff live them out, I was deeply comforted by the realization that God is in motion for me every day and is orchestrating powerful days for me.

— Geery Stolsfoos, Lead Pastor at Freedom Valley Worship Center,
   Gettysburg, Pennsylvania

Authentic, thoughtful, articulate, inspiring, empowering, innovative and solid are the first words that come to mind when I think of Jeff Leake. He's a leader I turn to when I need help processing complex leadership dilemmas. The powerful concepts he shares in this book have been tested over time in the lives of the effective leaders he has sent out. Read, apply, and grow!

— Steve Pike, Church Multiplication Network,
   Springfield, Missouri

I've had the privilege of knowing Pastor Jeff Leake for many years and on many different levels. He was my senior pastor, he has been a Metanoia Missions International board member, and he presently serves as part of our apostolic oversight for the Hosanna Network of Churches. In every role, and with every hat he puts on, Jeff remains solid and constant, continually exhibiting the qualities of a godly leader. Without a doubt, Jeff will continue to be a leading, influential voice in the church's future.

— Eric Ferguson, Founder of Metanoia Missions International,
   Findlay, Ohio

Father's Day of 1964 changed our lives forever when the author of *God in Motion* entered our home. I recall the joy of watching him take his first step physically. Greater joy entered my heart when I saw him taking his first step spiritually. When Jeff was a young man, we observed that God's hand was upon him and that He blessed him with great insight and extraordinary leadership gifts. I am confident that *God in Motion* will minister to you personally and provide a ministry tool to illuminate a welcome truth during difficult and discouraging experiences of those you love. Nothing happens to you by accident. God orchestrates and inserts plans and events for the accomplishment of His will and purpose.

— James Leake, President of Acts 20:24 Ministries,
   Monroeville, Pennsylvania

There's a reason that Pastor Jeff Leake is being asked to preach all over the nation. He is an exceptional communicator with a special touch of God on his life. In fact, he has started over fifteen churches in the past fifteen years. I have no doubt that God will speak to you and inspire you through this book.

— David Spencer, veteran missionary and board member of Church Growth
   International, Seoul, Korea

God in Motion

Making Sense of the Loose Ends in Life

Foreword by Scott Wilson

InfluenceResources.com

Published by Influence Resources
1445 N. Boonville Ave.
Springfield, Missouri 65802

Published in association with The Quadrivium Group—Orlando, Florida
info@TheQuadriviumGroup.com

Cover design by Keith Locke. www.keithlocke.com.

Interior formatting by Anne McLaughlin, Blue Lake Design,
Dickinson, Texas.

Unless otherwise specified, Scripture quotations are taken from the Holy
Bible, New International Version®. NIV®. Copyright © 1973, 1978, 1984,
2011 by Biblica, Inc. ™ Used by permission of Zondervan. All rights
reserved worldwide. www.zondervan.com

Scripture quotations marked (MSG) are taken from *The Message*, copyright ©
by Eugene H. Peterson 1993, 1994, 1995, 1996, 2000, 2001, 2002.
Used by permission of NavPress Publishing Group.

The author has paraphrased some passages of Scripture.

Note: The personal stories in this book are true, but in a few cases names
and details have been changed to protect anonymity.

ISBN: 978-1-93783-087-8

16 15 14 13 • 1 2 3 4
Printed in the United States of America

This book is dedicated to the love of my life, Melodie.
She is my best friend, my devoted encourager,
my partner in ministry, and the person who believes in me
more than I believe in myself.
Without her encouragement,
this book would never have been written.

Contents

Foreword

Today, a lot of people feel disappointed with God—and at some points in our lives, all of us feel that way. We've prayed for God to work in our marriages, but our spouses seem more distant than ever. We've pleaded with God to cause our children to walk with Him, but they're more interested in popularity than Jesus. We're burdened with worries about debt, our jobs, our parents, and our health. We've poured out our hearts to God, but the heavens seem silent. We want to shout, "What's the deal, God? Where are you? Aren't you paying attention to my needs?"

We're not alone. The prophet Isaiah recorded a time in the history of God's people when they were really disappointed with God. In fact, they'd given up on Him coming through for them. They were worried, anxious—and to be honest—pretty angry with God. The prophet responded with a pointed question and a reminder: "Do you not know? Have you not heard? The LORD is the everlasting God, the Creator of the ends of the earth. He will not grow tired or weary, and his understanding no one can fathom. He gives strength to the weary and increases the power of the weak" (Isa. 40:28-29). In a way Isaiah took the disappointed, doubting people by the shoulders, looked them in the eye, and said, "Hey, remember who you're praying to! God's not asleep. He's the loving Father, the glorious King, the One who is far wiser and stronger than you can imagine! He's the One we follow. He's the One we trust. Don't give up. Keep trusting Him!"

Then, Isaiah reminded the people of God's promise to come through, always—not necessarily in the way and the

14

timing they would like . . . but with the wisdom and strength they would need. In his most famous passage, Isaiah told them,

> But those who hope in the LORD will renew their strength.
>
> They will soar on wings like eagles;
>
> they will run and not grow weary,
>
> they will walk and not be faint (Isa. 40:31).

Will God come through? Absolutely. Will He do exactly what we want Him to do? Maybe . . . maybe not. The problem for many of us is that we insist that God fulfill *our* agendas, *our* plans, and that He meet *our* needs the way we want them met. Isaiah reminds us that God is God, the sovereign Lord of the universe. His understanding is inscrutable, and His plans are far greater than we can comprehend. He may not jump through our hoops, but He will always be faithful to accomplish His purposes—and His purposes are always good.

In this important verse about trusting God, modern translations use different words. Some say, "Those who hope in the Lord," but others say "wait" or "expect" or "trust." The Hebrew word means to twist, to tie, to form into a bond. Isaiah tells us that we need to wrap ourselves around the goodness and greatness of God. We need to remember His magnificent love, and not let anything pull us apart from Him—not worries, not doubts, and not delays. We talk often about "waiting on the Lord," but it's not really about time at all—it's about the expectation that the God of glory will show Himself strong and wise in our lives.

Another important word in this verse is "renew." We renew our hearts and our strength when we *take off* our attempts to get our way and *put on* God's agenda for our lives. We say, "Lord, I don't understand what's going on, but I trust you. You promised to work all things together for good in my life. I don't see how that's happening right now, but I trust you anyway. No matter what, I'm all yours."

The strength God provides isn't an ability to grit our teeth and work things out on our own. Isaiah is talking about the power of God's Spirit imparted to us and flowing through us—the same power that raised Jesus Christ from the tomb!

What can we expect when we wait and trust God in the midst of our difficulties? Sometimes, God works miracles that are so magnificent our hearts soar like eagles! Often, God gives us the direction and strength to run like we're in a marathon. Day after day, we get up with a purpose, and we see real progress as we love our spouse, help our kids grow up, care for elderly parents, see success at work, and trust God to use us to make a difference in the eternal destinies of people around us. But sometimes, the heartaches of life threaten to crush us. In those times, a genuine mark of the Spirit's presence and power is revealed in our ability to put one foot in front of the other. We aren't moving fast, and we can't see beyond the next step, but God gives us grace to do the next right thing.

In every situation of life, God orchestrates resources, provides truth, and sustains us with faith, hope, and love.

Trusting that God is always at work to fulfill His agenda is what this book is about. It's not a promise that God will fulfill *our* plans and dreams, but that He will lovingly remind us that His plans are best and His power is available. No matter what happens in our lives, we can trust that He's attentive, involved, and at work behind the scenes. Some of us need this reminder today. All of us need it from time to time.

I love Jeff Leake. I sense God smiles when He thinks of him, too. Jeff has a wonderful blend of kindness and strength, humility and vision. He delights in seeing people respond to God's grace. He and Melodie are a terrific couple, and God is using them in powerful ways.

If you talk to individuals who know Jeff, they'll tell you about his attentive love, listening ear, and genuine excitement about their lives. If you talk to his church leaders, they're thrilled to join hands with someone whose big vision and clear strategy are matched with authentic love for people. And now, I'm thrilled to say that God is giving Jeff a much bigger platform. He has never sought it, but leaders across the country and around the world recognize his warmth, insight, and spiritual power.

Jeff exemplifies the shepherd's care Paul described in his letter to the Christians in Thessalonica: "We loved you so much that we were delighted to share with you not only the gospel of God but our lives as well, because you had become so dear to us" (1 Thess. 2:8). People are dear to Jeff, and they know it.

As you read this book, I know you'll feel that Jeff is sharing his love and his life with you because he loves you. It's an honor to recommend Jeff to you. I'm sure God will use this book to warm your heart, build your faith, and give you a fresh sense of the Spirit's love and power.

Scott Wilson
The Oaks Fellowship
Red Oak, Texas

Acknowledgements

Many people have shaped my understanding that God is always in motion and working powerfully in my life. I deeply appreciate the ways they have contributed to my life, my faith, and my message.

My parents, James and Rebecca Leake, were the initial and primary lens through which I saw God's activity in the world. Their love for God's Word was contagious, and their testimony to the supernatural helped me see God in action.

Melodie's parents, David and Bonnie Spencer, have helped me see how God is always working to expand His Kingdom. I watched their bold aggressive faith as they stepped out to accomplish the vision God put on their hearts.

Allison Park Church has been the crucible where I've learned and experienced the lessons of this book. Our faith-filled pastoral team has encouraged my every step. The people of APC have always been willing to follow me as I attempted to follow Christ, even when the immense scope of God's vision has challenged our faith. My church family has been incredibly encouraging, devoted, and passionate about the presence and purpose of God.

Thanks also should go to many of the pastors who have planted churches over the years. I've learned through their experiences as they follow Jesus.

The influence of Johannes Amritzer is mentioned in these pages. He has had a profound impact on my view of Jesus. Johannes showed me that God is still at work in the same ways He acted through the lives of the apostles in the book of Acts.

Finally, I want to thank Pat Springle, who has helped put these words on paper. We discussed principles and themes I've taught for several years, dug into the Scriptures, debated how to communicate particular points, and looked for God in motion in the writing process. I appreciate Pat's contribution to the clarity and strength of this book.

chapter 1

Waiting on God?

God is always at work around us. Whether we
realize it or not, this is reality. . . . Reports of God
at work in the Bible are invitations for us to know
and experience God ourselves.

Henry Blackaby

I was frustrated! Can I be honest about that? I felt stuck.
I needed answers from God, but I heard nothing from
Him. The problem wasn't that I'd given up on prayer. I was
praying. In fact, I'd prayed about this specific situation hundreds of times. I'd even fasted and prayed for an answer.
Still, there was no response from God. No answer. No breakthrough. No peace.

I had a problem. I was working in an extremely dysfunc-
tional situation. I'd been an assistant pastor for two years in
a church that I loved, but the staff team had disintegrated
because of petty bickering. The dysfunction in our environment wasn't due to serious moral or ethical violations. No
one was fired for committing adultery or embezzling church
funds. Nothing had been done that would have made our

church the lead story on the local evening news. The decline began from a seemingly insignificant issue: Our staff team stopped resolving small disagreements. Like a corrosive acid, distrust and the unwillingness to forgive gradually ate away the network of our relationships. Soon, petty misunderstandings festered into bitterness, and people talked *about* people instead of *to* them. Instead of love, unity, and trust, we barely tolerated each other.

As these tensions rose, I asked God to allow me to pursue my dream, which was to identify a city in need and move there to plant a new church. As month after month passed, my anxiety increased. I begged God to release me from my assignment as the Assistant Pastor, but heaven was silent and nothing seemed to change. My utter frustration was compounded by an increasing workload. Several members of the pastoral staff had resigned (Why would they leave such a wonderful, positive place?), and many of their responsibilities were piled on my desk. To make matters worse, the staff that was left all went on vacation at the same time. My exasperation level reached a breaking point! Every day, I cried out to God for an open door so I could leave and start a new chapter in my life. Day after day, I prayed, but He seemed strangely mute.

One afternoon, as I drove home from an especially difficult day at work, the combination of fatigue and frustration boiled over. I let God have it! I prayed—if you can call it prayer. I shouted my anger at God. I screamed at the windshield, "God, this is totally unfair! I've been working like a dog. You know I want to leave here. This situation is ridiculous! I'm tired. I've done all I can, but it's not getting better. What's wrong? Why won't you open a door for me?"

After seething in silence for a few minutes, I exploded again, "God, I don't know how much longer I can take this!"

When I pulled into the driveway at our home, I felt mildly relieved that I'd vented my pent-up frustrations with God, but nothing in my circumstances had changed. I still had no peace, no direction, and no hope for change. To be honest, I felt God had abandoned me. He had put me in an uncomfortable place in my work life, and then He had walked away—or so it seemed.

The silence, though, was unbearable. I wondered if He was listening at all, and I wondered if He even cared.

At the time, I'm not sure I would have admitted it, but as I look back on my response to that painful experience, I have to confess that I believed I deserved better from God. I'd prepared for a life of ministry, I'd devoted myself to serve Him, and I was pouring out my life to help others. Surely, I deserved better treatment than this! If He wasn't going to give me a new direction, He could at least give me an indication of how long I'd have to endure this hardship. But my repeated requests seemed to bounce off heaven. If God had answered my prayers with "No" or "Wait" or "Do this" or "Don't do that," I could have accepted it. The silence, though, was unbearable. I wondered if He was listening at all, and I wondered if He even cared.

In my despair, I began asking a different question: "Why doesn't God want what I want?" This question led me to consider a different conclusion: If He doesn't want what I want, then, maybe it isn't that I need to try harder to get His attention. Do my desires, dreams, and expectations need to change? Maybe, the problem is me! I'd had an agenda for God, but He wasn't on board. Slowly, the idea formed in my mind and heart: I need to discover *His* agenda instead of insisting that He operate according to *my* timing and *my* plan.

At the time, unanswered prayer about my work situation seemed like the biggest problem in the world. However, since that day in the car, I've watched people encounter difficulties far more devastating than my uncomfortable work environment. I've watched single parents working hard to raise their kids in the hostile environment of a bitter custody fight. I've talked with people a few minutes after they've heard a diagnosis they never wanted to hear. Many men and women, young and old, have suffered from sexual or emotional abuse, abandonment, addiction, financial collapse, infertility, loss, natural disasters, and heartaches of every kind. When these unwelcome guests invade our lives, we instinctively ask hard questions, including "God, where are you?" "Why didn't you do something?" and "Can I ever trust you again?"

Honest to God

When we face tragedies and heartaches, we believe we have irrefutable evidence that God doesn't exist or that He doesn't care. Most of us would never voice this conclusion, and we're theologically sound enough to know neither is actually true. Still, in the depths of our souls, we may genuinely believe:

* God is *inactive*—so my prayers, fasting, and obedience must prompt Him to act.

* God is *unaware*—so my prayers must inform Him of the reality of my situation. Without my input, He's lost.

- God is *indifferent*–the intensity of my prayers must be the only hope to move Him to be compassionate and to act.

Doubt is insidious and deadly. We may try to convince ourselves we believe, but in reality, we completely justify our suspicions. For instance, if anyone had asked me during the time I screamed at God in the car if I believed He was inactive, I'd have given a theologically correct answer: "No, He's always at work" . . . then I would have muttered under my breath, "But I sure don't see it!" If a person had asked if I thought God was aware of my predicament, I'd have responded, "Of course, He's omniscient. He knows everything that's going on in the universe all the time." Then I would have muttered, "But *I'm* not silent when I notice people in trouble. What's going on with God?" And if anyone had asked if I felt God was indifferent, I'd have insisted, "The Father sent Jesus to demonstrate His love for us." Still, I would have wondered, "But where is He when I need Him?"

When we're pressed and stressed, the courtrooms of our hearts weigh the evidence and sometimes conclude, "On the charges of God being inactive, unaware, and indifferent, 'Guilty as charged.'"

If we believe God has abandoned us, we feel it's entirely up to us to get His attention and twist His arm to make Him take action. If we scream at the windshield and He doesn't show up, then we step into the street to flag Him down. A lot of misguided religious activity is designed for this purpose. We forget about grace. We conclude that our past is too shameful for God to come down to bless us or we're nobodies and He doesn't have time for us. We resort to one of two extremes: We either give up and quit pursuing God, or we double our efforts to get His attention. We pray, give, serve, and fast—not out of a heart of gratitude but to motivate God to get involved with our lives. When He doesn't give us what we expect, we don't know what else to do.

When we read the Scriptures, we find something shocking: Many people in the pages of the Bible had their own "screaming at the windshield" moments to tell God how upset they were with Him—and He didn't flinch. The Psalms are a holy collection of prayers and songs. Some of them shout praise to the wonder and majesty of God, some express heartfelt gratitude, but about half of them are "wintry." In these psalms, the writers pour out disappointment, anger, fear, confusion, and hurt. God doesn't blast them for being honest with Him. Quite the opposite, He invites them to be ruthlessly authentic. If we act like we're fine when we're dying inside, we shut off the opportunity to connect with God's heart. Authenticity enables us to build a relationship of trust and love.

> **If we act like we're fine when we're dying inside, we shut off the opportunity to connect with God's heart. Authenticity enables us to build a relationship of trust and love.**

Venting to God is a great start if we're going to break out of a cycle of despair and begin to understand Him and His plan. But we will never fully engage with God just by downloading our grief or questioning His methods. At some point, we need a paradigm shift, a radical adjustment in our thinking so we can see God from a new perspective. We need to see God for who He truly is. When we're frustrated, we're tempted to see God as *inactive, unaware,* and *indifferent.* Our painful and confusing moments seem to reinforce those ideas with hard evidence. In reality, God is exactly the opposite of what we feel. Indifferent? He cares more deeply about you than anyone ever could. Unaware? He knows every detail of your life, every detail of the past and every detail of the future. Inactive? Actually, God was working on your behalf before you were conceived. He is already working on things He has planned for you. He is constantly *in motion* preparing a future for you. But because His work is invisible to us, we often assume that nothing is happening.

In his letter to the Ephesians, Paul makes a radical declaration: "For we are God's workmanship, created in Christ Jesus to do good works, *which God prepared in advance for us to do*" (Eph. 2:10 emphasis added). Did you notice an important phrase in this verse? God has been working on you (His workmanship). At the same time, He's been working on your future (so that you could step into the good things He has prepared for you). He's not asleep, and He's not preoccupied. He's not twiddling His thumbs waiting for us to get His attention. He's been at work for eons to carefully orchestrate situations for His glory and our good. This encouraging statement, though, doesn't mean that life will be smooth and easy. God's purposes and paths *often* require perseverance and *always* require faith. In every situation— good times and bad, joy and grief—God is always at work.

Dread or Wonder

If we believe that the difficulties of our lives mean God is indifferent and inactive, we'll feel all alone. When we feel alone, we can become desperate. We think all the pressure is on us to figure out what to do. We try to force God to fix our problems. In fact, we believe that if we don't force His hand through our desperate pleas, He'll never act. Living with an inactive God leaves us with a nagging, gnawing sense of dread. However, if we believe God is always ahead of us, preparing circumstances and us for great things, we live with a sense of wonder at His greatness and grace. Even when we don't see what He's doing, we trust that He's good, His paths are right, and He's actively leading us. Life then is a treasure hunt, a process of discovery, and a thrill in following a God of infinite love, wisdom, power . . . and mystery. When we're amazed at God's grace and purpose, we keep our eyes open so we don't miss the wonderful things He has prepared for us. And even if we miss a few of them (and we will), God graciously weaves the loose ends of our lives into a beautiful tapestry of purpose, blessing, and love.

This insight changes everything—at least it did for me. When I was screaming at the windshield, angry and anxious because I didn't see any evidence of God's presence in my circumstances, I was miserable. Over the years, I've learned to trust that God is at work even when I don't see His hand at all. When I am confident that God is always in motion, I have peace in dark times, assurance when I encounter roadblocks, and great joy when I finally notice what He's been up to all along. For years, I believed that God had been in motion on rare occasions and during biblical times, but I didn't understand that God never stops working on my behalf. Maybe you've thought, *Man, it would have been great if I could have had a front row seat to observe the parting of the Red Sea or to watch the battle between David and Goliath. Those were the moments when God was really at work!* What I want you to consider is this: God is always at work—even in you and around you right now! And He's doing far more than you can imagine. He's extravagant, passionate, uncontained. If that's true, we should live with expectation and wonder about the present and the future.

> **What I want you to consider is this: God is always at work—even in you and around you right now! And He's doing far more than you can imagine.**

Ahead of Moses

As a young man, Moses had a plan, but he saw himself as the chief architect and power source. He was going to rescue God's people from their Egyptian slave masters. He didn't ask God for directions, and he didn't trust in God's leading. In his passion for justice, he murdered an Egyptian overseer who abused a Hebrew slave. Moses tried to keep the crime a secret, but everyone discovered his sin. Instead of being the champion of the Israelites, he was a chump. Forced to flee to the desert, he became an ordinary shepherd in the house of his father-in-law. For four decades, Moses' dream was dead. At eighty-years old, he lived with smelly sheep on the backside of nowhere. He thought his life was over.

Then God showed up.

As he tended sheep, Moses saw a bush that was on fire, but the flames didn't consume it. He went over to investigate. As he approached, God called him by name and announced, "Moses! Moses! . . . Take off your sandals, for the place where you are standing is holy ground" (Ex. 3:4–5). In this encounter, God told Moses that He hadn't forgotten him during all those lonely years. He still had a purpose and a plan for him. In fact, He had always had a plan.

God told Moses He was sending him back to Egypt to free the Israelites, but the man who had been impulsively bold forty years earlier had lost his confidence. He asked, "Who am I, that I should go to Pharaoh and bring the Israelites out of Egypt?" (Gen. 3:11) For a while, God and Moses debated the wisdom of sending a failed, aged revolutionary to complete a task that began with a false start so long ago. But God wouldn't take no for an answer.

From this encounter, we gain some important insights:

(1) God was in motion when Moses was confused and disillusioned.

For forty long years, Moses lived with nagging, painful memories of his failed attempts to deliver the people of Israel from their 400 years of slavery. He probably spent a lot of time wondering, *Where was God all this time? Why hadn't God acted?* Moses probably concluded that God had no role for him in any future plans. After all, he was eighty years old and was far removed from his days as a leader in Egypt. Moses may have assumed God was distant and dormant but, in fact, God had been in motion all those years behind the scenes. He hadn't forgotten His people who suffered in slavery, and He hadn't abandoned Moses. God had a bold and elaborate plan all worked out for Moses to follow. In their encounter, Moses voiced his doubts, but God met every objection with a clear answer:

Moses asked, "Who am I to do this?"

God answered, "I will be with you."

Moses wondered, "Who will I tell them is sending me?"

God responded, "I AM THAT I AM."

Moses inquired, "What if they don't believe me?"

God answered, "Throw down your staff and it will become a snake."

Moses complained, "But I'm not good with words."

God assured him, "I have made your tongue and can enable you to speak"

(Paraphrased from Ex. 3–4).

(2) God was in motion before Moses reached a conclusion.

Imagine being an eyewitness at this pivotal moment. God spoke to Moses out of a bush that burned but was not consumed. When God gave him directives, Moses had serious reservations. God directly answered all of his objections. The God of the universe had committed Himself to Moses. He assured him, "I, personally, will be with you. I am sharing with you my nature and my name (I AM), which has never been shared with anyone else." God didn't give Moses a single "sign" to prove His power and commitment. He gave three miraculous proofs: a staff that turned into a snake, a hand that became leprous and was healed, and the water of the Nile that turned to blood. But Moses begged God, "Lord, please send someone else!"

> It's challenge enough to believe that God will eventually act. But it's an even greater challenge to believe that God wants to act *through me*. At these crucial moments, my choice to believe involves *risk*.

I can identify with Moses' fears and doubts. Disappointments with life, with God, and with myself often leave me disillusioned. It's challenge enough to believe that God will eventually act. But it's an even greater challenge to believe that God wants to act *through me*. At these crucial moments, my choice to believe involves *risk*. Moses was haunted by his first attempt to deliver Israel, which ended in epic failure. Perhaps he concluded that since God hadn't backed him up when he tried the first time, why would God back him up now?

To address Moses' doubts, God gave him another miraculous sign—He had already sent someone to meet the need. The Bible says the Lord became angry with Moses. "All right," He said. "What about your brother, Aaron the Levite? I know he speaks well. And look! He is already on his way to meet you now. He will be delighted to see you" (Ex. 4:14 author's paraphrase).

I have to confess that I've read this story dozens of times without realizing the implications of this interaction. Do you see what God explained to Moses? God shared a little bit of what He had already been up to. Moses hadn't even agreed to the job God was calling him to do, yet God had taken the liberty to speak to his brother, Aaron, on his behalf. God explained, "He is already on his way to meet you now." Can you see the implication of this moment? God wasn't only working in Moses' life; He was working on *both ends* of Moses' life. On one end, He was speaking to Moses out of the burning bush. On the other end, He had *already* spoken to Aaron. God had prepared an answer to Moses' questions before Moses even thought of asking them. God had designed solutions for Moses' concerns before Moses even felt them. God had planned partnerships for Moses' future before Moses even understood what the future would hold.

For years Moses assumed that God was silent, but God was waiting for the right time to speak to him about the future. Moses believed God was dormant, but all along God had been planning and preparing the future. Moses felt as if God had abandoned him, but in reality, God had been walking with him and was planning on revealing Himself to and through Moses in a powerful way—so powerful that we're still discussing those interactions today.

(3) God was in motion during moments of great consternation.

I love the fact that God had already spoken to Aaron before He appeared to Moses through the burning bush. This gives us great assurance. It means that God is actively at work when we might assume nothing is happening at all. In fact, He's working on the other end of your life right now. There are people, positions, provisions, and partnerships being prepared for you even as you read these words. Remember Paul's assurance in Ephesians 2:10: ". . . for good works, which God prepared in advance for us to do." Those words "in advance" mean more than just that God is preparing things for us to experience. It also means that God is preparing things in advance of our understanding—beyond our comprehension. He doesn't tell us what He's preparing for us. He surprises us with it. Moses had no idea Aaron was on the way to meet him and become his partner in this call from God. That part of God's plan was invisible to Moses, but God was at work before and beyond Moses' awareness.

When God appeared in the burning bush, He reminded Moses of the plight of his people back in Egypt: "I have certainly seen the oppression of my people in Egypt. I have heard their cries of distress because of their harsh slave drivers. Yes, I am aware of their suffering. So I have come down to rescue them" (Ex. 3:7 author's paraphrase). How do you think Moses felt when God reminded him that his people were stuck in oppressive slavery in a foreign land? He may have felt ashamed, grieved, or angry. He may have wondered, *Where is God? Why hasn't He acted? Doesn't He care about His people? Isn't He aware of what's going on?*

God answered Moses, "I have heard! I am aware! And I'm coming to rescue!" God began to reveal the plan He had been working on all along. This should be a powerful encouragement to us. The fact that we can't see what God is doing right now doesn't mean He's not doing anything. He cares. He is aware. He is preparing the other end of our situations. He's doing advanced work right now. We can't see it yet, but it's happening. Of course, this assurance doesn't mean that everything about the future will be perfect. It doesn't make the painful moments of our past or present any less difficult, but it assures us that we aren't alone. No situation is hopeless—because God is present, aware, and involved.

How God Speaks

Some of us feel inspired by this encounter between God and Moses, but some of us feel deflated. We wonder, *So when do I get my burning-bush moment? It would be a little easier to accept this reality of a "God in motion" if I could have a profound experience and God offered real proof!* A burning-bush moment doesn't happen every day. In fact, as far as I know, it only happened once in all of history. The truth is that relating to an invisible, all-powerful God will always be mysterious. To impart His heart and His message to us, God has used a wide variety of methods, from a "still, small voice" to a blinding vision of the glory of God, from the gentle nudge of the Spirit to vivid dreams, from a roadblock to an open door. God isn't limited by time and space. He's creative, and He longs to connect with us. Most often, however, He uses His Word to share His mind and heart with His people.

To impart His heart and His message to us, God has used a wide variety of methods, from a "still, small voice" to a blinding vision of the glory of God, from the gentle nudge of the Spirit to vivid dreams, from a roadblock to an open door.

The challenge for each of us is to hold two seemingly opposite truths in each hand: to believe that God isn't distant, indifferent, or inactive even though He's invisible and inaudible. How do we find a God like that? How do we relate to Him? How does He communicate His purposes to us? We'd like to have the guarantee that God will show up in burning bushes in our lives, but the fact is that God never appeared to Moses in the same way again.

God knows each of us, and He knows the best way to get our attention and convince us of His love and purpose. It's His nature to be self-revealing. We may be slow to notice, and we may not like what we hear at times, but God delights in revealing Himself to anyone who wants to know Him. In the opening paragraphs of John's gospel, he calls Jesus "the Word." In first century Greek philosophy, *logos*, "the word," was considered to be an impersonal principle of reason. John used it in a very different way. When John wrote,

"In the beginning was the Word" (John 1:1), Jewish readers immediately thought of the opening lines of Genesis. There, God was the creative agent who formed the universe out of nothing. John was saying, "The one who created it all is the one I'm writing about in this gospel—it's Jesus Christ, the living Word of God." God isn't a distant creator; He's present, He reveals Himself, and He relates personally and intimately with His people.

I believe God specifically tailors His communication for each person, and He approaches each of us in different ways in particular seasons of our lives. We need never doubt that He's present, caring, and active. We don't have to wonder *if* He will connect with us, but the *how* and *when* of His communication is often puzzling. We may think that we really want to know God, but even more, He desperately wants to be known. He has gone to great lengths to reveal Himself to us. Jesus lived in glory, power, and wealth beyond imagining, but He "emptied Himself" and became a humble, poor servant—with no home, no money, and no possessions—to demonstrate His love for us.

The writer to the Hebrews gave us a glimpse of God's passion to connect with us by sending Jesus. He explained as follows:

> In the past God spoke to our forefathers through the prophets at many times and in various ways, but in these last days he has spoken to us by his Son, whom he appointed heir of all things, and through whom he made the universe. The Son is the radiance of God's glory and the exact representation of his being, sustaining all things by his powerful word. After he had provided purification for sins, he sat down at the right hand of the Majesty in heaven (Heb. 1:1–3).

What is God like? How does He want to relate to us? The answer to these questions lies in the life, heart, and actions of Jesus Christ. When we read the gospel accounts, we see what thrilled Him and what made Him angry, what moved Him to tears and what compelled Him to sacrifice His life. Do you want to know God? The author of Hebrews says, "Look to Jesus. He's the exact representation of the character and heart of God." If God would go to such incredible lengths to become a human being to relate to us, can't we assume He longs to share His heart with us today?

Of course, this assumption takes faith. If we're yelling at the windshield because we haven't heard anything from God in a while, we need to back up a little and say, "Maybe . . . just maybe, God is already in motion, but I haven't seen Him yet. Maybe I can trust that the God who loved me enough to come to earth and die for me hasn't abandoned me after all. Maybe I can trust Him to work." As we cling to this ray of hope in the middle of our doubts and confusion, we may realize our perspective needs some adjustment. We may have been expecting Him to fulfill *our will*, but He's waiting on us to long for *His purposes*. There can be a difference . . . a big difference, and the delay may be God's way of refocusing our priorities.

When I insist that God reveal Himself in a certain way at a certain time to fulfill my wishes, I'm usually disappointed. Often when I hear people tell stories of how God worked in their lives, I assume He has the same plans for me. But comparison like that destroys. It destroys our openness to the wonder and creativity of God. Over the years, I've learned that there are no formulas to show us how to relate to the God of the universe. Principles? Yes. Stories? Certainly. But even a casual reading of the Bible shows a vast array of ways God shares His heart with human beings.

The Thrill of the Unknown

When we look closely at the life of Jesus, we find a beautiful and complex character. He was as tough as nails and incredibly tender, a fierce defender of those who were oppressed, and a delightful friend. He was decidedly different. He said and did things that confused people, yet He was supremely approachable. It seemed that no one could really get a handle on Him. His words and actions often perplexed even His closest friends. I get the idea that the disciples got up every day and asked themselves, "Well, I wonder what in the world is going to happen today!" They were seldom disappointed. In contrast, what does it mean for us to follow Jesus today?

Jesus Christ was many things, but He was never boring. I think of Him as wild and good—someone who amazes me, challenges me, and thrills me.

Is there a sense of adventure? Too often, Christians have done something His most bitter critics never could accomplish: We've made Him boring. Jesus Christ was many things, but He was never boring. I think of Him as wild and good—someone who amazes me, challenges me, and thrills me.

Over the years, I've been learning an important lesson: When it appears that God isn't paying attention, I can be sure He's about to do something wonderful. My first glimpse into this principle of spiritual life occurred during the time when I was in the car yelling at God. Shortly after that, God opened a door I had no idea existed. If I'd gotten my way and God had fulfilled my agenda, I would have missed the most amazing things God has given me to do. Let me put it this way: If God had given me what I wanted, I would have regretted it for the rest of my life. As I look back, I wonder what my "batting average" was during that season of my life. Did my desires line up with God's will half of the time? A third? A tenth? Today, I hope my desires are more in alignment with His agenda, but I'm sure I still miss some things He wants for me. More than ever, I want what He wants to be what I want, but I'm realistic about a flawed, finite human being trying to relate to an infinitely wise, good, and powerful God.

And for You

As you read this book, I hope God gives you a fresh, new perspective about Him and your life. To some degree, all of us come to God with our own agendas. Slowly, gradually, and wondrously, God softens our hearts, changes our perception, and shares His heart with us so that His agenda becomes ours. God is already at work to shape your life. In fact, He's been engineering circumstances since the beginning of time to capture your heart and give you a desire to honor Him. Look for Him and pursue the adventure of knowing and following a really good and really wild God.

Matthew records two short parables that Jesus told about people finding something incredibly valuable. In the first story, a man walked through a field and noticed a chest containing a priceless treasure. Jesus said, "in his joy [he] went and sold all he had and bought that field." In the second story, a man searched diligently for the finest pearls.

One day, he found one of startling beauty. This man, too, made a dramatic choice: "He went away and sold everything he had and bought it" (Matt. 13:44-46).

In these stories, both men found something of great value. One accidentally stumbled on it, but the other had been looking diligently. In both cases, what they found captured their hearts. They "sold everything" to possess the treasure and the pearl. In these stories, the treasure and the pearl represent Jesus. No one demanded that these men sell their possessions to have the treasure and the pearl. No one had to use guilt to force them. The value was so great that giving up everything was the only reasonable response.

Do you and I believe Jesus is that valuable? Is He a treasure worth more than all the possessions, positions, and popularity the world offers? Or do those other things still seem more important? If we insist on a manageable, safe, predictable God, we'll have only a caricature of the real thing. There's only one God, and He waits for us to discover Him in all His glory, mystery, and tenderness. Don't settle for anything less. It's the greatest thrill you'll ever experience.

At the end of each chapter, you'll find some questions. Take time to reflect on these and write your answers. Then, if you're in a Bible study class or discussion group, share your thoughts with one another. God will use your conversations to sharpen your thinking and deepen your faith.

Consider This

1. When was the last time (or the most memorable time) you felt exasperated with God and told Him so? How did you feel when you told Him?

2. What are some circumstances that may cause someone to conclude that God is distant, indifferent, and inactive?

3. Can you think of some Psalms in which people poured out their hearts to the Lord? What emotions did they express? How did they find hope and help?

4. Read the story of Moses and the burning bush in Exodus 3. How do we see that God was already in motion before this encounter?

5. How does it help to realize that God is in motion in our lives before we see His hand at work?

6. What are some ways God speaks to people? What is the way He most often communicates with you? How do you normally respond?

7. Do you see God as "wild and good"? How would it affect your relationship with Him if you did?

8. What do you hope to get out of reading this book?

chapter 2

A King with His Sleeves Rolled Up

I need to worship because without it I can forget that I have a Big God beside me and live in fear. I need to worship because without it I can forget his calling and begin to live in a spirit of self-preoccupation. I need to worship because without it I lose a sense of wonder and gratitude and plod through life with blinders on. I need worship because my natural tendency is toward self-reliance and stubborn independence.

John Ortberg

The city of Pittsburgh has always been identified with the steel industry and its National Football League team, the Steelers. My city has a reputation for being a gritty, tough town. The football team, like the city, has always exemplified this blue-collar mentality. The Steelers are known for their hard-nosed, knock-you-down, stop-you-at-any-cost, "steel curtain" defense and a rugged, smash-mouth running game on offense, nothing flashy—just rough, strong, resilient, defiant strength. In fact, the Steelers are the only team in the league with no cheerleaders. It's just not our style.

When the steel industry was at its height, chimneys belched smoke from huge factories. Under the mammoth roofs, men in protective gear poured molten steel at about 2,500 degrees. Almost every man who worked in these conditions bore the scars from the searing liquid splattering and finding a gap in the protective clothing. A few men fell into the cauldrons. They didn't last long.

If you stood outside the gates of the steel mills a few minutes after the whistle blew and the shifts changed, you'd see people walking out who had done the hottest, hardest, most dangerous work you can imagine. Like the football team, the look on their faces revealed nothing flashy—just resilient, defiant strength.

How does the God of the universe relate to people like this? Wasn't Jesus sweet and mild? Is there any connection at all between Jesus' life and the real-life challenges experienced by these hard-working, blue-collar steel workers? Does Jesus understand the rigors of real life? Can God relate to the hot, intense, wearisome trials that people endure throughout the world today? Can Jesus relate to me?

The Bible tells us that Jesus grew up and labored at a job much like these steel workers' jobs. Most people think of Him working in a carpenter's shop, but the term in Greek that we define as "carpenter" was the same term used for stonemasons. The lack of availability of wood in the region where Jesus lived means He probably pounded rock as often as He cut wood. He lived in Nazareth, a backwater village in Palestine—nothing fancy, nothing notable. Until He was thirty, Jesus hauled rocks or pounded nails. He sweat, and He met deadlines. Every day He put in a full shift of hard labor. When He got home each evening, He plunked down His lunchbox and sat to rest. He was bone tired.

When God showed up in human form, blue-collar men and women would have understood Him. The people coming out the gate at the steel mill would have looked at Him and thought, "He's one of us." He was born to poor teenagers, laid in a feeding trough, and surrounded by stinking animals. His birth was announced only to lowly shepherds. Eventually, His family moved to Nazareth where He learned a trade and became a stonemason. Can you see him? Muscular . . . sinewy . . . sweating.

Is that the image you and I have of Jesus? It's not the common conception of Him. Throughout the last two millennia, artists have depicted Him as a bit effeminate, with a halo over His head and an otherworldly expression on His face. Steel workers would have little respect for a God like that. I realize I'm on thin ice with people who love the traditional iconography of a sweet Jesus who carries lambs and floats a foot above the ground, but my reading of the Gospels paints a different picture. The King of the universe came with His sleeves rolled up.

Beyond 2D

When the image of Jesus in our minds remains two dimensional, we miss the dynamic person He is. We don't have relationships with cardboard cutouts. We relate to people: We love them and laugh with them; we hurt them, and they hurt us. When Jesus remains a flat, abstract concept, the Christian faith is only a nice set of stories and recommended principles.

Melodie and I have been married for twenty-five years. I'm sure

> When Jesus remains a flat, abstract concept, the Christian faith is only a nice set of stories and recommended principles.

I still miss some cues, but over time, I've picked up some patterns in her personality. I know she likes plenty of cream and two sweeteners in her specialty coffee. I've learned that she really doesn't like it when I make fun of her in public. In fact, I know the look on her face when she thinks I've crossed that line. I may think it's funny; she doesn't. I can anticipate what will make her laugh, and I know her favorite color is green. I know these things—and countless others—because Melodie is a person, and we have a real relationship. People relate to each other like this.

God invites us to relate to Him in the same way. He has preferences and feelings. Sometimes He's delighted; sometimes He's grieved or angry. He invites us to understand His heart and identify His values. He has a history and a story. In fact, His story is more thrilling, dangerous, and intriguing than any Bourne movie!

We read about Him in a Bible that was written thousands of years ago, but He's not relegated to the distant past, like Alexander the Great or Charlemagne. And He's not a mystical principle or a set of noble concepts, like Buddhism or Confucianism. God is far greater than we can ever imagine—the Alpha and the Omega, the creator of all—but He's as close as our breath. He's a friend to sinners like you and me.

When I read the four gospel accounts of the life of Christ, I'm struck by what's *not* included. The writers focus on the miracles, teaching moments, and debates, and, of course, all four give special emphasis to His death and resurrection. But anyone who knows how men operate realizes the writers didn't describe most of the "down time" Jesus had with His disciples. The narrative says they were at the Sea of Galilee, and then we see them in Jerusalem. A map and timeline of the ministry of Christ shows how far they traveled. They didn't go by jet or bus or car. They walked everywhere they went. As they walked along, they talked, asked questions, and laughed. Around campfires each night, they told stories and probably poked fun at each other. Behind, beneath, and around all the situations described in the Gospels were countless hours when Jesus' followers spent uninterrupted time getting to know Him. They were eyewitnesses of His public ministry to heal lepers, raise people from the dead, teach on hillsides, hug children, weep at gravesides, restore sight to the blind, feed thousands with a boy's sack lunch, and debate angry religious leaders. But they also got to see a side of Jesus the crowds never saw—the private, unguarded moments on the roads, in homes, and around campfires. In those times, I'm sure He shared His heart even more.

The disciples had a special opportunity to know Jesus, and they quickly realized He was no ordinary person. Time after time, they marveled at His actions and His words. When they were caught in a storm on the sea, even the experienced fishermen among them feared for their lives. Strangely, as the waves rocked the boat, Jesus stayed sound asleep. They woke Him and shouted, "Master, Master, we're going to drown!" Jesus woke up, analyzed the situation, and promptly told the wind and waves to be quiet. No problem there. Luke may have had a smile on his face when he wrote, "In fear and amazement they asked one another, 'Who is this? He commands even the winds and the water, and they obey him'" (Luke 8:24–25).

The disciples knew Jesus as a person. They knew how He liked His fish prepared, what made Him laugh and cry, and what cares tugged on His heart. That's why it hurt Him so much near the time of His arrest when Thomas and Philip proved that they didn't really understand Him after all. Jesus told them, "I am the way and the truth and the life. No one comes to the Father except through me. If you really knew me, you would know my Father as well. From now on, you do know him and have seen him."

Philip, though, didn't get it. He asked, "Lord, show us the Father and that will be enough for us."

We can hear the pained exasperation in Jesus' reply, "Don't you know me, Philip, even after I have been among you such a long time? Anyone who has seen me has seen the Father. How can you say, 'show us the Father'?" (John 14:6-9)

When someone we love and trust doesn't understand us, isn't this how we feel, too? Don't we want to say, "Have we been married (or friends or co-workers) this long, but you still don't understand me?" That's how Jesus felt. He had poured out His heart for them, time after time, and He was about to empty His life for them. He hoped for more from their relationship.

Why is it so important to understand Jesus from this "reality-based" perspective? Because when we believe in anything other than the "real person of Jesus" we believe in something false. We can't make up what we want Jesus to be like! He's not one thing to one person and something completely different to another. He's a person, which means that He's unique. When we understand who He really is, we can worship Him in spirit and in truth—intimately and accurately. Worship or allegiance to anyone or anything other than the true God is idolatry. But when we know what Jesus is like, we get our best picture of what God is like, because

Jesus is the "exact representation" of God (Heb. 1:3). Everything we need to know about God begins and ends with Jesus.

We can know the heart and character of God by looking at Jesus. We know what God values by observing what Jesus valued. We know what makes God happy or sad by seeing what thrilled Jesus and what made Him weep. Jesus didn't sit and wait for people to come to Him. He was active, always in motion, moving toward people in need—and even toward controversy. Why? So He could care for the hurting, correct false teaching about God, and resist evil. The gospel writers, especially Mark, communicate a sense of urgency in Jesus' actions. In dozens of passages, Mark tells us Jesus acted "immediately." He's still doing those things today in your life and mine. He still has a sense of urgency. He's always in motion.

The King's Plans

When Jesus came to earth, He came with a primary message. He came declaring, "The Kingdom of God is near." We all know the nature of earthly kingdoms, but the authentic Jesus we read about in New Testament history came to bring a new Kingdom to the earth—and He is the King of that Kingdom.

Kings rule. They reign over kingdoms. As King, Jesus is "far above all rule and authority, power and dominion, and every title that can be given, not only in the present age but also in the one to come" (Eph. 1:21). As His subjects and friends, we pray, "Your kingdom come, your will be done on earth as it is in heaven" (Matt. 6:10). That's His agenda, and it's up to us to get in line with His purposes, His plans, and His heart.

The values of God's kingdom are different from the values of governments, companies, and most people. In fact, His is an *upside-down* kingdom. He avoids the things most people pursue and pursues the things most people avoid. Jesus painted a picture of this upside-down kingdom in the Beatitudes (Matt. 5:3-12):

- Most people long for wealth and power, but Jesus said, "Blessed are the poor in spirit."

- People pursue pleasure at all costs, but Jesus said, "Blessed are those who mourn."

- We marvel at powerful, beautiful people who rise to the top, but Jesus had the opposite value: "Blessed are the meek."

- All around us, people grasp for more power, popularity, and possessions, but Jesus said, "Blessed are those who hunger and thirst for righteousness."

- Many people only feel confident if they jockey for position so they can be one-up on their competitors, but Jesus said, "Blessed are the merciful."

- We often wink at sin and make jokes about people who make hard decisions to do what's right, but Jesus said, "Blessed are the pure in heart."

- People love to find fault in others, to put them down so they can feel superior, but Jesus said, "Blessed are the peacemakers."

- Today, people assume they have the right to comfort, ease, and prosperity—especially if they're Christians—but Jesus said, "Blessed are those who are persecuted because of righteousness. . . . Blessed are you when people insult you, persecute you and falsely say all kinds of evil against you because of me."

These statements aren't isolated concepts in the Bible. We find the upside-down kingdom described in many different ways. If we let them sink in, all of them make us shake our heads to be sure we've heard them right: the first shall be last and the last first; if you want to be great, become the servant of all; to experience real life, you have to die to yourself; those who insist they see are really blind, but those who admit they're blind have real perception; the way to true honor is through humility; to become mature believers, we have to trust God with the faith of a little child; to win the applause of God, we serve in secret; and when we're weak, we're strong. We aren't on our own to muster up these perspectives. We look at Jesus. He is the awesome King who became poor to make us rich, suffered humiliation to provide us with an honored place at His side, and died to give us life.

God's values are counter-cultural. They go against the grain.

God's values are counter-cultural. They go against the grain. If we follow Him, we stand out—as lightning rods for criticism and as lights on a hill to show the way. The world's pursuits promise peace, glory, and power, but they inevitably result in broken relationships, shame, and emptiness. When we have the courage to follow the King, however, He promises different results: the joy of being His partners, comfort, a wealth beyond bank accounts, the fullness of the Spirit, mercy, a rich relationship with God, a new identity as His sons and daughters, and a prophet's reward.

Jesus is a unique king. Pharaohs, ancient monarchs, Roman emperors, and kings throughout history ruled with ruthless power and demanded that others bow to them. *Jesus served.* In fact, He served to the point of death. For Jesus, there was no kingdom without a cross. The crucifixion—a humiliating, excruciating, public death—launched His kingdom on earth.

Believers have always had a hard time understanding the upside-down nature of Christ's kingdom. Prestige, popularity, power, and possessions are attractive to us, and we assume God's job is to provide them for our pleasure. We're not alone in making this glaring mistake. When people were slow to catch on to Jesus' purpose, James and John reacted with ferocity, "Lord, do you want us to call fire down from heaven to destroy them?" (Luke 9:54) And later, on the night He ate with His disciples before He was arrested, Jesus took time to explain the radical nature of the new kingdom yet again in these words:

> The kings of the Gentiles lord it over them; and those who exercise authority over them call themselves Benefactors. But you are not to be like that. Instead, the greatest among you should be like the youngest, and the one who rules like the one who serves. For who is greater, the one who is at the table or the one who serves? Is it not the one who is at the table? But I am among you as one who serves (Luke 22:25–27).

We need a new set of lenses so we see God, ourselves, and everything else with spiritual clarity and focus. Then we'll learn to value humility, kindness, and forgiveness instead of insisting on our own way and getting back at those who hurt us. We realize God's kingdom is invisible, but it becomes visible in the lives of those who love and follow Him.

God has put the desire for Him and His kingdom in the heart of every person. Our desires are twisted by sin and channeled in wrong directions, but at the core of our hearts, we know we can't be satisfied by anything less than knowing the King and joining Him in changing the world. All around us, people are trying to fill their lives with substitutes. They hope these things can bring ultimate fulfillment, but they can't.

In a poignant, accurate, and brief statement, St. Augustine sums up man's search, "You have made us for yourself, O Lord, and our hearts are restless until they rest in you."[1]

Jesus is the dividing line of history into BC and AD, but He's also the dividing line in every person's heart. When we read the Gospels, we can observe widely varied responses to Him. Some people hated Him, some feared Him, and some adored Him, but no one simply tolerated Him. He was too much of a lightning rod for that. In our churches today, however, many people walk in and out each week only slightly

In our churches today, however, many people walk in and out each week only slightly entertained by what they've heard, read, and sung. When this happens, it's obvious they haven't encountered the real Jesus.

entertained by what they've heard, read, and sung. When this happens, it's obvious they haven't encountered the real Jesus. I'm not blaming pastors (though sometimes, we may be unclear), and I'm not saying that each person is hopelessly selfish (but we're all afflicted with that disease). Whatever the cause, the failure to realize who Jesus is creates all kinds of troubles.

When we follow the King, we notice what He did and how He did it. Then, and only then, can we imitate Him in every possible way. After describing what it means to live by the grace of God, Paul gives a summary: "Be imitators of God, therefore, as dearly loved children and live a life of love, just as Christ loved us and gave himself up for us as a fragrant offering and sacrifice to God" (Eph. 5:1-2). We become more like God when we imitate Jesus in love, humility, and sacrifice.

We can't serve Him or others, though, unless we're the grateful recipients of His loving service to us. We can't draw from an empty well, and the well can only be filled with the genuine experience of His grace and power. The Creator of the universe came to this world to serve people, including you and me. He pursued us even when we didn't care, and He poured out His life for us even when we were ungrateful. We can't twist His arm to get Him to accept us—grace means that He loves us and accepts us in spite of our sins.

The more I read and study about Jesus, the more I'm amazed at who He was . . . and still is today. He moved toward overlooked people who were outcasts and the dregs of society: lepers, demon-possessed people, crippled people, blind people, prostitutes, women, children, and hated Samaritans. But He didn't despise the rich and popular. He met with Nicodemus, one of the religious rulers, to explain spiritual life to him. When He approached Jericho, He saw Zacchaeus sitting in a tree. Zacchaeus was a man of fabulous wealth, the chief tax collector who extorted money from his countrymen for the Romans. In this role, he was considered a traitor. Others despised him, but Jesus loved him. Jesus reached out to both the down-and-out and the up-and-coming. His love included Mary Magdalene, who was possessed by seven demons, and the rich young ruler, who seemed to have it all together. No one was beyond His love.

A Tailored Approach

It's striking to me that Jesus didn't have a standard approach when He encountered people. I'm not against Christians learning a technique to communicate spiritual truth, but Jesus tailored His approach to each person. The way He talked with the woman at the well was different from the way He talked to Nicodemus or the woman caught in adultery or the leper. He still tailors His approach today. He's amazingly creative. The God of the universe has entered time and space to restore a relationship with each human being. He knows what's in every person's heart, and He's well aware of everything in our backgrounds. It shouldn't be surprising that He carefully crafts His words and methods to get the attention and capture the heart of every person.

My friend Johannes Amritzer is an Austrian who currently lives in Sweden. He was raised in a family steeped in chaos. His father was a boxer who was often in and out of prison on various charges, and his mother was an alcoholic. When his father was away, his mother's boyfriends beat him. When he was six years old, Johannes was placed in a

foster home. On the first night, they led him into the base-
ment and showed him his new bed. He was terrified, and he
missed his mother. After a few minutes, a thirteen-year-old
boy, who was also a foster child, came down the stairs and
sat on his bed. He gave Johannes a glass of milk and told
him stories until he drifted off to sleep. Every night, the boy
came down to comfort him.

When Johannes tells this story, he says that the older boy
was an example of Christ's love. Somehow, the boy realized
the little kid downstairs felt afraid and vulnerable. He could
have stayed upstairs and played with the older children, but
he took the initiative each night to comfort a boy he had
never seen before. Later, Johannes became a Christian, and
he realized that Jesus steps into our lives at our point of desperate need, fear, and vulnerability to connect with us in a
personal way—much like the older boy in the foster home.

More than anyone else, Johannes has taught me that
Jesus Christ is a real person who wants to relate to me. I'm
a pastor's kid who grew up in church, but the way Johannes
talks about Jesus touches me deeply. As I look back now, I
previously thought of Jesus in the abstract—a person who
lived long ago, a force, a set of truths, a path to follow. But
Johannes has shown me a vital, personal, approachable
Jesus who delights in my response to His initiative—just as
Johannes' friend delighted to see him when he came down
the stairs each night. When Johannes talks about Jesus, He
seems to leap from the pages of Scripture, and I'm more
aware of His presence throughout my day.

Several years ago, I went on a mission trip with Johannes
to Harar, Ethiopia. The city is 98 percent Muslim. We held
an outdoor gospel festival in the city, and we encountered

persecution. On one of our outreaches into the villages, someone threw a rock at one of the men traveling with us and fractured his skull. The experience was intense, but our purpose was to declare the person of Jesus to a Muslim city that was opposed to our theology. I was intrigued by the strategy Johannes employed. When he preaches in countries that have little or no Christian heritage, he talks little about the process of salvation. Instead, he preaches about the person of Jesus—which is how Peter and Paul preached in the book of Acts: Jesus was God in the flesh; He performed miracles, died, rose from the dead, and ascended back into heaven. In Ethiopia, as Johannes declared the fact that Jesus is alive and available to every Muslim who chooses to believe, God released a wave of miraculous power. On the second night of the festival, a man who worked at a local gas station came up to the front. Everybody knew him. He was deaf and mute. The Holy Spirit touched him, and in front of the audience, he heard and spoke his first words.

Word of the healing got around town, and the next night, a crowd packed the place! Suddenly, I realized that the living, loving Jesus wanted to show Himself to these Muslims. We weren't talking about the idea of Jesus; we were talking about having a personal encounter with Him! On that night, Johannes preached about Jesus as the deliverer. In the middle of his message, he said, "I call out every demon in this place; I cast you out in the name of the risen Jesus Christ." As soon as the words were out of his mouth, about twenty people began to shake violently. Demons were manifesting as they came out of those who were possessed. Now, let me assure skeptical readers that no one in Harar had watched Christian television. They had never seen any of the activity that often goes on in a charismatic Pentecostal environment. They weren't mimicking things they'd seen somewhere else. No one was faking being demon-possessed. This was the real thing!

Our people carried those who were possessed back to a tent so they could minister to them. I didn't want to miss this, so I followed them. I watched as person after person was set free by the cleansing blood and the power of Jesus Christ. It was, I realized, exactly the way Jesus had cast out demons in Palestine—same problem, same person, same power. In Luke's introduction to his history of the early church, he explained that Jesus died and was raised from the tomb. After the resurrection, He "showed himself to these men and gave many convincing proofs that he was alive" (Acts 1:3). In the Muslim city of Harar, Jesus was doing the same thing—giving the people many convincing proofs that He was alive!

He is active, constantly in motion, working to accomplish His kingdom purpose in and through your life.

After Jesus rose from the tomb, the Jewish leaders tried to assure everybody that He was still dead and the disciples had stolen His body. For forty days, Jesus proved them wrong. He appeared to individuals, small groups, and more than 500 people at one time. And after several weeks, He ascended into heaven and now sits at the right hand of the Father. But make no mistake about it: This same Jesus is alive today. He is aware of what's happening in your life. He cares about you. He is active, constantly in motion, working to accomplish His kingdom purpose in and through your life.

Before my experiences in Harar, my concept of Jesus was cloudy. Now He has become *real* to me. I admire Him, and I love Him. He's my hero and my friend. He's not just a theological construct. I love Him and everything about Him. I'm amazed by His humility, and I'm in awe of His courage. If you like gripping stories about real heroes, read about Him in the Gospels.

In the opening of his gospel, Mark described a situation when Jesus met a leper. The man had probably been an outcast for many years. When he discovered his disease, the priest sent him away from everyone he loved. He could no longer provide for his family, which left his wife and children destitute. His family members couldn't contact him, and he was shut off from society and worship. No one had hugged him since the day his skin started rotting off. In that day, it was assumed that sickness was always the result of sin, so in addition to his physical pain and family estrangement, he felt the wagging finger of condemnation from other people.

When Jesus approached him, the man took a radical step. He broke from the confines of his quarantine and threw himself in front of Jesus. Even though the leper was looking directly at God in the flesh, he was still unsure about the same questions that haunt us today. Does God care? Is He indifferent to my needs? Is He aware of what I feel and what I've experienced? The leper spoke to Jesus, "If you are willing, you can make me clean." It's my observation that most people don't doubt God's ability. The man didn't say, "If you are able, you can make me clean." The question is never really about the ability of God—we question the *willingness* of God.

How did Jesus respond to this question? Mark described what happened next: "Filled with compassion, Jesus reached out his hand and touched the man. 'I am willing,' he said. 'Be clean!'" (Mark 1:41) My first response to this description is to ask, "How did Mark know Jesus was 'filled with compassion'? How can you read compassion on someone else's face?" There's one way that is fairly clear. You can read compassion when you see tears. I believe Jesus stood weeping over the man and his condition.

As He met the leper that day, the carpenter-stonemason, sweaty, blue-collar guy was the King with His sleeves rolled up. He was strong . . . but amazingly tender. In an instant, He understood this man's situation: the pain, the shame, the fear, and the thread of hope. Jesus didn't stand back and heal the man from a distance. He did the unthinkable— through His tears He reached out and touched the man's rotten flesh.

In this account, the healing is secondary to me. What's important is that Jesus wept over this man and touched him. What is God like? How do I know what He feels about my situation? All I have to do is look at Jesus. He cares for me in the same way. He approaches me, sees my filth and smells my stench, weeps over my hurt, and reaches out to touch me. When I'm at my worst, Jesus already knows everything I'm going through. When I scream at the windshield, Jesus doesn't turn away in disgust. He's right there . . . caring, loving, and healing. He's as approachable as a best friend on a camping trip, but He's the sovereign Lord of all. That's the King I want to follow. That's the King I love and admire. That's the King I've given my life to.

Can you imagine how this story ended? Jesus cleansed the leper by a word. He said simply, "Be clean." The man went away cleansed, healed, and restored. Imagine when he returned home after the priest checked him. His family saw him coming down the front walk, but they couldn't believe their eyes. Daddy was home, and he was healed! No more leprosy—no longer quarantined and unemployable. No longer called "unclean," which was how they described the shame of being sick. Theologically, they believed that sickness was a direct result of someone's sin. Jesus rejected that idea. He touched the leper. He cleansed him, restored his body, and gave him back his dignity. Because of the active, compassionate response of Jesus, this man once again had a family and a future.

The Source

In our spiritual lives, it's easy to miss Jesus. We tend to substitute rules, rituals, and religious experiences for the genuine adventure of being in relationship with Jesus Christ. We often judge our success as a Christian by how much we know about the Bible, or by the number and intensity of our spiritual and emotional experiences, or even by how many good things we've done for other people.

Reducing the Christian life to things like these is like pouring molten steel on a cold slab. The love and joy go out, and we're left rigid, judgmental, competitive with others, angry with God, and cool in our worship. There is only one standard of measure for success as a Christian: how much a person becomes like Jesus. He is the pinnacle of our focus. He reveals God to us, and as we follow Him, He forms the character and nature of God in us.

We need to keep looking to Jesus as our great, loving, compassionate King. Knowing and loving Him is not about raw emotion or following rules. Life with Him is about majesty and mystery. We learn that He's fully capable of doing anything, but His paths are sometimes baffling. Like the characters in great stories, we follow a hero into uncharted territory. From time to time in the story we face cliffhanger moments. We aren't sure which way to go or how to get out of a predicament, but in the nick of time, the hero shows up again.

What does it mean to know Jesus? We get a glimpse when we read the opening chapter of Revelation. John was perhaps Jesus' best friend on earth. He was close to Jesus at the Last Supper, and he was the only disciple who had the courage to show up at the cross. Many years later, John was an exile on the island of Patmos. There, he had a vision of the risen, glorified Christ. The scene was so overwhelming that John fainted! The awesome King tenderly reached out and touched His friend, comforted him, and gave him a message and a mission (see Rev. 1:10-20). When we look at Jesus, what do we see? How do we respond? If we aren't amazed, we're not looking at the real Jesus. If we don't sense His tender touch, we don't understand His kindness. If we don't realize He's given us a mission to fulfill, we're just being entertained by our religious practices.

Following King Jesus is the most exciting adventure the world has ever known. There are few guarantees about the path—only that He's already in motion ahead of us. This confidence inflames our worship, deepens our devotion, and directs our requests. Actually, if we aren't expecting a lot from God, we don't really know Him. John Newton was the captain of a slave ship when God turned his life around. He became one of the greatest champions of God's "Amazing

Grace." Newton, who wrote that famous hymn, understood that grace leads us into a vibrant faith in the greatness of God and makes us confident that He can do big things. He wrote another song titled, "Thou Art Coming to a King." Here's one stanza:

Thou art coming to a King,
Large petitions with thee bring;
For His grace and power are such,
None can ever ask too much;
None can ever ask too much.

When you come to King Jesus, don't be shy. Come boldly to His throne of grace. There you'll find a treasure chest full of purpose, power, and love. You'll never be able to understand Him fully, put Him in a box, or control Him. He's much too big and mysterious for that. Our King is awesome beyond telling and incredibly tender. He's worthy of our love and obedience.

Are you following Jesus like this? If not, don't try to muster up the emotions, and don't try to follow enough rules to earn His acceptance. Dig deeper. See yourself as the hopeless leper Jesus touched through His tears. See yourself as the self-righteous Zacchaeus, whose wealth couldn't mask his deep need to be forgiven. See yourself as the prostitute who was so thrilled to be loved and forgiven by Jesus that she barged into a dinner party to bathe His feet with expensive perfume and sweet tears. You and I are those people. When we grasp this fact, we'll love Jesus more than anything, and we'll obey Him out of thankful hearts.

Be Sure

Maybe you're new to the pursuit of spiritual life, and this picture of who Jesus really is inspires you and makes you long for more. Or maybe you've been in church for many years, but the description of a real relationship with God causes you to realize something is missing. Some of us know a little about God's grace, and we may have felt close to God at one point in our lives, but now, we aren't so sure. But we *can* be sure.

The Bible says, "Everyone who calls on the name of the Lord will be saved" (Rom. 10:13). Jesus didn't say, "Grab a ticket to heaven," and He didn't tell us to pray a prayer. Over and over again, He invited people by saying, "Follow me." When we realize Jesus is real and alive, we open our hearts to Him. He wants to take away our sin, cleanse us, liberate us, and make us His own. He's our King, who has proven He's worthy of our affection and obedience. Following Him isn't drudgery, and He doesn't force us to come along. He gives us a gracious invitation to be forgiven, to be healed, and to join Him on the greatest adventure of our lives. It won't be easy, but it'll thrill our hearts and challenge our socks off!

Follow Him. Let Him be your hero, your North Star, and your best friend. Let Him change your heart so you have some of His compassion and His courage. Invite Him to have full reign in your life, over your relationships, your habits, your finances, and your dreams. Does this sound scary? Of course it does. He wants nothing less than everything we've got. But here's the thing: we can trust Him with every fiber of our lives.

Salvation is much more than escape from hell. When we say yes to Jesus, we experience the wonder and adventure of following the King.

Consider This

1. How might it affect a person's faith to see Jesus as the sweet, mild guy holding a lamb? Or as an angry judge finding things in us to condemn?

2. What difference does it make to see Him as a blue-collar carpenter or stonemason—the King with His sleeves rolled up?

3. Describe the upside-down kingdom. Why is it so counter-intuitive for many Christians?

4. What stories in the Gospels (such as Jesus touching the leper) help you see Him as both amazingly powerful and tenderly compassionate? How do these stories affect your relationship with Him?

5. How would you describe the effects of the two opposite mistakes in our relationship with Christ: focusing too much on emotions or too much on rules? Has either of these been a problem for you? Explain your answer.

6. In what ways is following the King a thrill? In what ways does it threaten us?

7. Is it possible for a person to be sure he or she is secure in a relationship with God? If not, why not? If so, what is the source of this certainty?

chapter 3

Junior Partners

**The two most important days of your life are the
day you are born and the day you find out why.**

Mark Twain

A few years ago, I was on a flight home from Denver to
Pittsburgh. I'd been gone for a week—a week packed
with meetings, services, and conversations with friends. I was
bone tired. I got a nice surprise when I got to the gate that
day. I had enough frequent flier miles to earn an upgrade
to first class. I was finally "one of those people" we all view
with a hint of envy (okay, maybe more than a hint) when we
board a plane. When I sat down in the lush, spacious seat, I
thought, *Thank you, God! This is just what I need.* I'm not sure
I actually prayed this next part, but I certainly thought, *I hope
the guy next to me doesn't want to talk. I'm too tired for that.*

After a minute or two, I noticed that the man sitting
next to me had a strange bag under the seat in front of him.
I looked a little more closely and saw a nose. He saw me

looking, so he said, "That's my dog. I travel with him everywhere. Don't worry. He won't bother anybody."

I nodded. As far as I was concerned, that was the end of our conversation. A few seconds later, I realized he wanted to talk. He began telling me the story of his life. He was a Jewish businessman from Pittsburgh. I tried to give plenty of signals that I didn't want to get into a three-hour conversation, but he didn't pick up on my subtle cues. He told me about himself, and then he began a series of questions about me. After a few about my family and where I lived, he asked, "What do you do for a living?"

I've been around long enough to know that when I say, "I'm a pastor," the whole conversation gets weird in a hurry. Some people assume I can fix all their problems, and others assume I'm the cause of all their problems. There was no way out. I looked him in the eye and said, "I'm a pastor."

He took a deep breath that was almost a groan, and then he replied, "Oh, I *can't stand* you people!"

I'd had plenty of people raise their eyebrows when I told them my profession, but I'd never had anyone be so instantly dismissive. I asked, "What do you mean?"

He answered, "You're all gun-toting, ultra-right-wing Republicans. That's what I mean."

I bristled, "Sir, you don't know me. You don't know my politics or anything else about me. How can you assume to know who I am and what I believe?"

He launched into a long discourse about his perspective on life, his view of God, and his prejudices about narrow, self-righteous Christians—especially pastors. After he talked for a long time, I decided not to defend myself because it would only enflame the discussion into a full-fledged argument.

I told him, "Sir, I have to say that I admire you. I have the greatest respect for the Jewish faith and traditions. The part of our Scriptures called the Old Testament, your Bible, contains some of the most amazing accounts of God working in, for, and through His people. Again and again, God intervened in human history. He showed up and did incredible things. These stories inspire me and build my faith."

He shook his head and muttered, "I don't believe any of that stuff."

I was only mildly surprised. I replied, "Really?"

"Yeah," he continued. "I think God created the universe, set it spinning in space, and hasn't touched it since."

I gently answered, "I don't see God that way at all. The accounts in the Scriptures—and in the lives of people today—show that He's personally engaged in our lives and very active." I tried to push back a little. "All the stories—Abraham, Moses, the Exodus, David and Goliath, and all the others—don't you believe they happened?"

"No, they're just myths or legends—stories people made up along the way."

I wasn't finished, but I changed course. I asked, "Do you celebrate Passover each year?"

He perked up a little. "Yes, our family celebrates Passover."

"So," I kept at it, "Passover is a powerful celebration of the moment in time when the Creator God intervened on behalf of the people of Israel to deliver them from slavery in Egypt. Do you believe God showed up to rescue His people and lead them through the desert to the Promised Land?"

He thought for a few seconds, and then he said, "Yeah, that might be one time God actually showed up. Maybe that one's true."

I told him, "Please, consider this: If God did it once years ago, maybe He's still active in people's lives today."

He nodded that I might have a point. Then I explained, "I think God showed up most dramatically in human history when He came to earth in the form of Jesus Christ. He demonstrated His presence, His power, and His love through Him." I paused to let that point sink in, and then I continued, "There's no pressure. You don't have to believe what I'm saying, but I want you to know that this is what I believe very deeply."

He sat back in his seat, thought for a long minute, and then looked back at me with a smile. He said, "You know, you're not a bad preacher after all. Where's your church? I want to hear you speak someday."

Before this conversation began, I had every intention of avoiding everyone and anyone around me on the plane. But God had other plans. If the man next to me hadn't had that little dog, we may never have started talking. And if he hadn't pursued me by asking questions, I'd have quickly retreated into silence. God, however, was already moving in this man's life and mine. He put us in seats next to each other, and He prepared both of us to talk about the things that matter in life. I was willing to be God's partner at that moment—just barely willing—but that was enough for God to use me to plant a seed of the gospel.

I had assumed my move to first class was for my comfort, but it had a different purpose: God's divine appointment. I suspect this happens more than we know. We move along through our day while God is orchestrating situations and preparing people for us to touch their lives—if we're willing to join Him.

One of the First

One of the most astounding facts of our faith is that the King invites us to be His partners in His great work of redeeming people and restoring the world. We're His partners, but make no mistake—we're junior partners. We're like the mouse in the story of the elephant and the mouse. After they walked across a bridge and made it sag and groan, the mouse turned to the elephant and said, "Man, we really shook that bridge up, didn't we?" Or, it's like the comment by Stacy King of the Chicago Bulls after a particular game when he commented, "I'll always remember this as the night Michael Jordan and I combined for 70 points." Jordan had scored 69 of them.[2] Yes, we're partners with God, but we need to have the right perspective.

Jesus modeled this partnership in His ministry and His approach to life. The gospel of John gives us a great example. Jesus and His disciples were taking a shortcut through Samaria on their way from Judea north to Galilee. On this part of the journey, they were in hostile territory. The Jews and the Samaritans traditionally hated each other. They approached the town of Sychar near midday when it was hot. The disciples went ahead to find something for lunch while Jesus sat near a well.

Soon, a woman came to the well to draw water for the day. This was odd. Women went to the well early each morning with their friends. It was as much a social occasion as a chore, much like friends going shopping together today.

On the surface, this interaction didn't hold much promise: a tired, hot, hungry Jewish man and a Samaritan woman who looked strangely out of place. When we're uncomfortable, all we can think about is instant gratification and relief.

In fact, we often measure how much God loves us by our current level of comfort. If we're not happy, it's God's fault.

Jesus saw the situation through a different lens. He noticed that this woman was strangely out of place, and He assumed the Father was at work. He initiated a conversation with her and exposed a far deeper problem than an empty water bucket. She had huge holes in her heart because of painful, disappointing relationships. She had been married and rejected five times. Now, she was living with a man but wasn't married to him. She was considered the village tramp. In that day, women had little means of economic support. To survive, they depended on a husband. This woman had been married five times. Five men had proposed, but all five eventually divorced her. When Jesus met her near the well that day, she was carrying years of rejection, shame, self-loathing, and guilt. But the Father in heaven saw her and loved her, so He designed a divine appointment for Jesus.

I find it incredibly touching that God saw this woman's sad predicament and designed something wonderful for her.

I find it incredibly touching that God saw this woman's sad predicament and designed something wonderful for her. Everyone in her village whispered about the immoral woman who couldn't keep a man. She was relegated to draw water at noon, the hottest part of the day, in order to avoid the stares and the derogatory remarks from the other women in town. If anyone was unworthy, it was this woman. But God looked down, saw her pain, and loved her. Jesus came into the world specifically for people like her, and the Father designed this moment for her rescue.

Jesus started the conversation with a simple request, "Can I have water?" His request triggered a barrage of objections from her. First, Jews and Samaritans didn't speak to each other. Second, who was He to offer her water? Was He greater than her forefathers who dug this well? Third, they each had a very different theology. Which was the correct place of worship: that mountain or the Temple in Jerusalem?

Often, intellectual questions are attempts to shield us from the greater questions that weigh deep on our hearts.

Finally, Jesus pointed out this woman's problem. He instructed her, "Go, call your husband." She responded, "I don't have a husband." Jesus answered, "I know. You have had five, and the man you are living with now is not even respectful enough to marry you.' She was startled by Jesus' insights into her life. She responded, "I see you are a prophet." Jesus then challenged her, "The kind of worshippers the Father seeks are those who worship in spirit and in truth." The combination of that statement and Jesus' earlier offer to give her water that would quench her soul for eternity must have hit home with her. Her decision of surrender to God isn't recorded in John's story, but the next time we see her, a crowd of people are following her from her village. She has recruited them all to follow her out to the well to see this man "who told me everything I had ever done." A village revival occurred as a result of Jesus' interaction with this one very sinful, very damaged soul (John 4:1–42).

Jesus didn't arrive at Sychar with an elaborate strategy to reach the city. He and His men were just passing through. (If I'd been in charge of creating an evangelistic plan for that city, I probably wouldn't have picked the town's outcast as the principle spokesperson.) Jesus simply saw what the Father was doing, and He stepped into that moment. He observed a person in need and assumed that His Father was at work. He simply took the step to join the Father. His decision to step into a divine appointment released an explosion of opportunity and ministry. The divine moment was spiritually, emotionally, and relationally transforming for the woman, and it was fulfilling to Jesus. In fact, being the Father's partner was so fulfilling to Jesus that when His disciples offered Him lunch, He told them, "I have food to eat that you know nothing about. . . . My food is to . . . do the will of him who sent me and to finish his work" (John 4:32, 34).

A little later in John's gospel, Jesus explained His ministry strategy: "I tell you the truth, the Son can do nothing by himself; he can do only what he sees his Father doing, because whatever the Father does the Son also does" (John 5:19). Jesus was always looking for the Father's signals. In fact, if you look through the Gospels, you'll see that most of the interactions Jesus had with people were actually divine interruptions. He didn't plan to be in a boat in a storm, to have crippled people need His help in the synagogues, to be asked by a Roman centurion to heal his servant, to encounter a woman burying her dead son, to find a demon-possessed man living in the tombs, to have a sick woman touch the hem of His cloak, to have blind men yell at Him from the side of the road, to be asked by a synagogue official to heal his sick little girl, and here, to find a lonely, foreign woman drawing water in the middle of the day. All of these events and many more were divine interruptions. All of them were signals that the Father was already at work preparing people for a supernatural, life-changing encounter with Jesus. In fact, we don't ever see that Jesus was surprised by these interruptions. He expected these signals because He knew that's the way the Father works. He understood that the Father is a God who is always in motion—never inactive, unaware, or indifferent.

God gives us signals, too. When we experience discomfort, instead of being myopic and focusing only on meeting our own needs, we can step back and look at the bigger picture. We can assume God is already at work, and He's inviting us to join Him in something special. Interruptions and discomfort are often clues that God is at work. We need to pay attention. God is on the move.

Interruptions and discomfort are often clues that God is at work. We need to pay attention. God is on the move.

If God is fully attentive, actively engaged, and always working around me, it would be silly for me to fail to notice Him—and fail to even look for Him. When we notice and take steps to solve the problems He shares with us, we develop a deeper intimacy with God. We experience more of His heart, and we sense more of His pleasure. We know we're doing what He has created us to do, and we're thrilled that He has chosen us to join Him.

We get to know people at a certain level by meeting to talk over coffee, but our understanding and appreciation of people multiplies when we work side by side with them. We not only hear their words, but we also see their responses to difficulties and opportunities. We share laughs, and we sweat together. These active interactions deepen relationships and build far stronger bonds. A team of people in a company works hard to craft a business strategy and implement it.

When a platoon goes into battle, they "have each other's back." Each of the eleven men on a football team has an assignment on a particular play. If anyone doesn't do his job, the play will fail. Even when it succeeds, each person hits the person across the line and is hit by players from the other team. Executing the play, whether it achieves success or failure, is a shared experience that forges individuals into a real team. The principle that "active participation produces deeper intimacy" works in every kind of human relationship: in families, at work, in the military, through sports, in churches, and on mission trips.

In the same way, we get to know God at a certain level in times of personal devotions, Bible reading, and prayer. We know Him a bit more in corporate worship. But we connect with His heart far more intimately when we're active partners in His efforts to redeem souls and restore relationships. As we weep, laugh, and sweat with Him and other believers, our hearts sing like Paul's at the end of his prayer recorded in Ephesians: "Now to him who is able to do immeasurably more than all we ask or imagine, according to his power that is at work within us, to him be glory in the church and in Christ Jesus throughout all generations, for ever and ever! Amen" (Eph. 3:20–21).

When I came back from Harar with stories of how God had included me in His work, I almost exploded with excitement! Words came in torrents of vivid descriptions. The look on my face showed people that this experience had gripped my heart. I told everybody who would listen (and maybe a few who didn't want to hear it again). I was like the obnoxious young man who is so in love that he can't stop talking about his girlfriend. It was like my team had just won the Super Bowl! I was no longer just going through the motions, and I didn't approach my personal devotions as a dry ritual. I didn't read the Bible as a manual to help me become a better person so I could get ahead or impress people. Suddenly, God was far more real, and my life was far more meaningful than it had ever been before. In Harar, God and I had been "in it" together. He and I had shared experiences and a common story. I was aware of Him in ways I hadn't been before, and I fully expected Him to show me many, many more opportunities to join Him in His gracious work. More than ever, I was stunned by Jesus—His tenderness, His amazing strength, and His incredible offer to forgive any sin and restore every heart.

Throughout the Old Testament, we find many different names for God. Each of these came out of an experience of seeing God act with power and grace. Each one reminded the people they could trust Him the next time they encountered difficulties. For example, when God gave Abraham a ram and stopped him from sacrificing his son, God was called Yahweh-Jireh, "The Lord will provide." When God's people won a battle over the Amalekites in the desert, they called God Yahweh-Nissi, "The Lord our banner, or the Lord our warrior who fights on our behalf." When David considered the constant care of God, he called Him Yahweh-Rohi, "The Lord our shepherd." Each name highlights a particular aspect of God's character that we come to know by experience. Some things, we know logically and conceptually, and we describe people and events based on rational observations. But God can't be contained in a single name or adjective. He's much too grand, glorious, and mysterious for that! He's awesome beyond our imaginations, but He delights in making

Himself known to us, and He invites us to be His junior partners. When we accept our roles, we get to know Him from an entirely new vantage point. We get to know Him in a working partnership. Amazing!

From looking at Old Testament stories of God's interventions and Jesus' encounters with people in the gospel accounts, we notice a distinct order of events—an order we can trust, see, and follow:

- God is already at work to prepare people and circumstances.

- We keep our hearts and eyes open to notice needs and opportunities.

- We join God in answering questions, meeting needs, and touching hearts.

- We know and love God even more because we've seen Him at work through us.[3]

The truth is that God is a terrific leader, but He's a terrible follower.

From these points, some people might conclude that I'm against plans, strategy, and preparation. Those who think that's what I'm suggesting don't know me very well! Planning certainly isn't wrong. It's good and right to chart the course for our days, our weeks, and our lives, but we need to be open to God's surprise interventions. We often assume, "I'll make my plans, and God will bless them. That's the way life should work." Woody Allen reportedly said, "If you want to make God laugh, tell Him your plans."[4] The truth is that God is a terrific leader, but He's a terrible follower. He's the King; we're not. He's the sovereign Lord of the universe who knows all things from beginning to end; we often don't know what's coming up in the next minute. When we're not open to God's interruptions, we miss out on part of the adventure of following Him, and we miss opportunities to be His partners in changing lives. Each day, we need to wake up and pray, "Lord, I have some plans for today, but you're probably going to interrupt them with something better—far better. Open my eyes to the opportunities you put in front of me today. I don't want to miss a thing!" That's a totally different way than most people view their days, their agendas, and their lives.

"I Have a Problem"

One day, I was complaining to God about all my needs, the needs of my church, the needs for the future. I created a long list of all the things I wanted Him to do for me. I insisted that His decision to answer my specific requests was the best course of action we could pursue together. The problems I was bringing before Him seemed so huge, so urgent, and so necessary. Then the Spirit whispered to my heart, "Have you considered that I have problems, too?"

I was surprised and a bit confused. "What?" I prayed. "You have problems?"

As I thought about it, I realized that the items on God's list are very different than the ones on mine. All of a sudden, my mind and heart were filled with the awareness of hurting people I had visited recently in my own city. I was reminded of the faces I'd seen in third-world nations on my mission trips. From the vantage point of heaven, God sees

the injustice of millions of people caught up in human trafficking, of crippling diseases around the world that result
from people drinking dirty water, of millions who are political and religious refugees, and the list goes on. I suddenly
realized my "desperate needs" by comparison weren't so important after all.

What does it mean that "God has problems"? It doesn't
mean that God has issues that He can't resolve or impossibilities that He can't overcome. It means He has burdens
on His heart. God cares deeply about people and situations.
He hears their cries and wants to rescue them. He wants to
restore broken families and heal broken hearts. He wants
to protect the vulnerable and help those who are in need.
When I stopped to think about these things, I didn't feel
like God was overlooking me at all. Instead, I realized He
was inviting me to join Him in solving His problems. He was
calling me to have His heart for people, to care like He cares,
to weep like He weeps, to rejoice like He rejoices, and to be
His partner. King David wrote, "The LORD confides in those
who fear him" (Ps. 25:14). When God shares His problems
with us, He's confiding in us as trusted friends, beloved children, and valued partners.

When God asked me if I'd ever considered if He had
problems, I had to stop and reflect for a while. I realized
I'd been looking at the world through the wrong end of the
telescope, and everything but me seemed really small. Suddenly, God flipped the telescope around, and the things on
His heart became large to me.

I realized that people pray desperate prayers every day
and hope God hears their cries. God listens, and He wants
us to join Him in answering those prayers. However, if we're

too focused on our own problems, we won't be aware and we won't care about the needs of others. In his book, *You Were Born for This*, Bruce Wilkinson describes a reality that was new to me—we are "God's miracle delivery system."[5] When God acts in the world, He primarily uses us as His instruments of peace, pardon, power, and purpose. He could use pillars of fire and smoke or some angelic messenger or supernatural tool. Instead, He gives us the unspeakable dignity and high honor of being His hands, feet, and voice to right wrongs, care for victims, and restore hearts.

All over the world—and all around our community—people are waking up and begging God to restore their marriages, bring their prodigals home, give them enough to eat, and lead them to jobs so they can provide for their families. In contrast, many Christians wake up and pray, too, but their prayers are often small prayers: "Lord, it's so hot. Will you bring a cool front," or "God, if you love me, give me a parking place at the mall near the door."

We have a choice. We can be God's partners and participate in solving problems that are on His heart by being miracle delivery systems, or we can be self-absorbed and worried about our own desires.

We have a choice. We can be God's partners and participate in solving problems that are on His heart by being miracle delivery systems, or we can be self-absorbed and worried about our own desires. Don't get me wrong. I'm not saying our needs aren't important—to us or to God. But I'm suggesting that if our hearts are aligned with God's, we'll imitate Jesus by caring more for the needs of others than for our own needs. Jesus "emptied Himself," took the form of a bondservant, and died for those He loves. Maybe we could make a bit more room in our hearts, in our prayers, in our spending, and in our time so we could join Him in caring for others. Instead of praying, "Feed me. Comfort me." we could learn to pray, "Lord, trust me with the concerns on your heart. Release resources to me and point me to people who need to be fed. Give me the ability to bring comfort to those who are hurting." When we see ourselves as God's partners, we'll experience the thrill of seeing Him work in us and through us to change the world, one person at a time. There will be a cost, and we'll face risks. Is it worth it? Each of us has to decide. I'm in. How about you?

An Active Agenda

I love to body surf when I go to the beach. I paddle out past the point where the waves are breaking, and I look for the next set to come to shore. As I'm waiting, I stand, holding onto the board. I keep an eye out behind me to see the next wave, in front of me to make sure no one is going to drop in front of me, and beside me to be sure I have enough room to maneuver on the wave. I'm in a posture of readiness. I'm aware, eager, and excited about catching a great wave. I try to catch the wave at its maximum height and velocity. The feeling of riding a good wave is exhilarating! I love it.

There's a big difference between riding a huge wave and paddling into shore because you missed the last good set of the day. Many people miss the waves God puts in their lives. We try to do all the work ourselves and wear ourselves out trying to make things happen for God, rather than waiting on God to carry us with velocity and force toward the destiny He has in mind for us.

Too often we substitute our own efforts and agendas for His. God is strategic and omniscient. He doesn't come up with His ideas on the spur of the moment. He's been planning things before time began. Many of life's events may seem random and even chaotic, but God orchestrates His plans carefully to the second. His infinite wisdom creates His plans, and His infinite love directs them.

We get a glimpse into His plans when we realize the Bible uses two distinct words that are translated as "time." *Chronos* is the ticking clock, the succession of one moment after another. We get our word *chronology* from it. *Kairos* is a precise moment, due season, "the fullness of time."

Paul explained to the Galatians, "But when the time had fully come, God sent his Son" (Gal. 4:4). The Father had been arranging the conditions of the birth of His Son for thousands of years prior to the moment of His birth. Seconds had ticked. Minutes had progressed. Hours had become days. Days had turned into weeks and years. Time had passed (chronos). Hundreds of years had passed, and still the Jewish people were left wondering when God was going to fulfill His promise to bring the Messiah into the world to be their Savior and Deliverer. Chronos time had passed, but nothing seemed to be happening. Yet all the time God was working behind the scenes to align people and situations to create the perfect setting for the birth of the Messiah.

Suddenly, Jesus was born. It occurred "at the right time" (kairos). It was the divine intersection between what seemed to be an ordinary moment (chronos) and what became a divine, world-altering moment (kairos). Jesus was born in Bethlehem, which fulfilled prophecies about where the Messiah would be born (Micah 5). He was born in the right place because a pagan Emperor was in power to call a census to prompt Joseph (who was from the proper Jewish genealogical line) and Mary (who was also from the proper genealogical line) to travel to Bethlehem during the ninth month of her pregnancy. The Father planned it with incredible precision.

God is still weaving chronos and kairos together. When I got on the plane to fly back from Denver, my watch showed chronos time. But God changed my seat to first class so I could (reluctantly) enter a conversation with a Jewish man about the Messiah. That wasn't an accident. It was kairos, a moment orchestrated by the God of the universe to accomplish His divine purposes.

The challenge is to "see the unseen," to believe that God is at work when we can't detect His hand at all, and to look for Him every time something or someone breaks into our day.

Every day, God has an active agenda to bring kairos into our chronos. We may carefully pray and plan to fulfill His will, but we also experience many divine interruptions. The challenge is to "see the unseen," to believe that God is at work when we can't detect His hand at all, and to look for Him every time something or someone breaks into our day.

Paul understood that God is just as hard at work in our lives as He was in Jesus' life. He concluded, "Let us not become weary in doing good, for at the proper time [kairos] we will reap a harvest if we do not give up" (Gal. 6:9). Don't give up. Keep trusting, keep looking, and keep joining Him when you see Him at work.

Be Ready

What does it mean to be God's partner? How can we get ready to join Him? I believe we need four essential ingredients: potential, preparation, perception, and posture. Let's look at these:

Potential

Our lives aren't just about accumulating more stuff, having a good time, or surviving the day's troubles. We're built for more than this. We were created to participate in the greatest adventure known to man and to join with the God of the universe each step of the way. Sometimes, people talk about this person or that one having "potential." They usually mean he can hit a ninety-mile-an-hour fastball, she has leadership skills, or he's got a great personality and would be a good catch. God sees us with far more potential than that. If we put our hands in His, we have the unspeakable opportunity and challenge of changing the eternal destiny of countless people, bringing justice and mercy to those who have lost hope, and caring for those who feel forgotten.

Preparation

We are God's masterpiece. Before time began, God began preparing situations for us and us for the situations. He doesn't just show up at a moment in time. For countless centuries, He's been carefully orchestrating people, circumstances, governments, families, births, deaths, hopes, dreams, and every aspect of human life to put us in the right place at the right time in the right frame of mind. Each kairos moment is a divine collision between God's work to prepare us . . . and His work to prepare the person in front of us. In

God's sovereignty, everything matters. In fact, the painful circumstances we've experienced are all part of God's grand design. If we let Him, He'll use every sin to give us a deeper appreciation of His grace, and He'll use every hurt to create compassion for others who suffer. In God, nothing is wasted. Like a master builder or chef, He uses every ingredient in His creative process to produce something beautiful and delicious.

Perception

Our challenge is to avoid being preoccupied with all the things that might be on our agenda. If we're not careful, we won't see the opportunities God has put in front of us. We need spiritual, expectant eyes to notice each moment—especially times of tenderness, heartache, frustration, or fear—as an open door that we can walk through to join God in touching lives. He's always at work. How often do we notice?

We naturally avoid pain at all cost, but human suffering is a magnet that attracts God's attention. When we realize this, we'll have a different perspective about the pain we encounter—in our own lives and in the lives of those around us. C. S. Lewis observed, "God whispers to us in our pleasures, speaks in our conscience, but shouts in our pains: it is His megaphone to rouse a deaf world."[6]

Hurting people felt drawn to Jesus, and even those who opposed Him knew it. At one point, He went to a synagogue on the Sabbath. A man with a withered hand was there that day. Jesus' enemies "watched Him closely." They knew that Jesus' attention would be drawn to the person in the room with the greatest need. They also knew it was the Sabbath, and it was against the traditions of the religious Jews to do work—like healing—on the Sabbath (Matt. 12:9-14).

Jesus' enemies had a close eye on the man in pain because they knew Jesus would focus on him. Jesus always places His attention on the person in the room who is hurting the most. So, if you wonder where God is at work at any moment, look for people in pain. Certainly, God is already at work to meet their needs. When we put our attention where God is already working, we often find an invitation to join Him in His work.

Accurate perception comes from looking three ways: We look back, look up, and look out. We *look back* to notice how God has worked in our lives. For instance, if we've struggled with bitterness, but God has given us grace to forgive those who have deeply wounded us, we can be sure He's preparing us to help someone else whose resentment is poisoning his life and relationships. We *look up* at the King to see Him in all His tenderness and strength. He's not like anyone we've ever encountered

When our hearts break over the needs of others, it's a sure sign we've been captured by the love of Jesus.

before! He is both the Lion of Judah and the Lamb of God. When we look at Him, we're amazed. And we *look out* to see people the way He sees them. Bob Pierce is the founder of World Vision, an organization that cares for desperate needs in third-world countries. On his first trip overseas, he encountered a sick child. He suddenly felt overwhelmed with Christ's compassion for the child. He prayed, "Let my heart be broken by the things that break the heart of God."[7] When our hearts break over the needs of others, it's a sure sign we've been captured by the love of Jesus.

Posture

When we grasp the principle of pain, we get ready to ride the wave of the Spirit. If every time we see a person in need, we think, *This is probably a God-moment,* and we pray, "Lord, what do You want me to do?" we're ready.

A man in our church (we'll call him Bill) was a waiter at a nice restaurant. Another waiter, Scott, got stiffed on a large bill. The restaurant's policy was that waiters were responsible for any checks that weren't paid. Scott was barely making it each month. He simply didn't have the resources to pay it, so he expected to lose his job. Bill noticed Scott's point of need, and he realized God had put him at that spot at that time for a reason. Bill went to every waiter, explained the predicament, and asked if they'd pitch in to help pay the bill. Everyone was glad to contribute—some a lot, some a little. Scott was so moved by Bill's loving initiative that he asked, "Can I talk to you?"

Bill nodded, "Sure."

After work that day, the two men sat in Bill's car in the parking lot. Scott poured out his heart. He said his wife had left him, and he was struggling to raise their son. Bill told Scott about the love and forgiveness of Christ, and Scott trusted the Savior. A few weeks later, Bill had the privilege of baptizing his friend at our church.

When the party left the restaurant that night without paying the check, Scott was shattered. Bill noticed his need. Bill didn't have enough money to pay the whole bill, but he had enough love to find the resources. The stiffed check, though, was just a small piece of the puzzle God was putting together in Scott's life. It was a flash point, a moment of need, the kairos when God stepped into his life in partnership with Bill.

Are you ready? Has God been tugging on your heart as you've read this chapter? I hope so. I have a lot to learn, but I'm totally committed to sharpening my spiritual vision so I notice more of what God is up to all around me each day.

Consider This

1. How do you normally respond to interruptions?

2. In what ways might pain and discomfort be signals that God is at work?

3. What are some of the problems on God's heart? How do you know? Which of these capture your attention? Explain your answer.

4. How does it change your self-perception to realize you're "God's miracle delivery system" for people in need?

5. Explain the difference between chronos and kairos. What are some examples of God working "the fullness of time" in the Bible and in your life?

6. In what way is pain "God's megaphone to arouse a deaf world"? How has God used pain to get your attention?

7. What are some ways you can improve your spiritual posture so you can be ready to ride the wave of the Spirit?

8. Each day this week (and maybe for the rest of your life), pray, "Lord, I have some plans for today, but You're probably going to interrupt them with something better—far better. Open my eyes to the opportunities You put in front of me today. I don't want to miss a thing!"

chapter 4

First Things First

The reason why many are still troubled, still seeking, still making little forward progress is because they haven't yet come to the end of themselves. We're still trying to give orders, and interfering with God's work within us.

A. W. Tozer

When Sarah showed up at our church, her life was in shambles. Her husband had threatened to leave her, but the state beat him to it. He was arrested on drug charges, convicted, and sent to prison. Sarah had two young children in junior high school. This little family was trying hard to make it through each day. Even from prison, her husband sent angry, scolding, threatening letters. If anyone had a right to be angry, it was Sarah, not her husband. Her husband had been a serial adulterer, a drug addict, a pusher, and he had been violent in the home. Like many women from abusive homes, she felt the strangely conflicting emotions of hating him and longing for him—and then feeling guilty and foolish.

It was easy for me to notice Sarah, even the first week she came to our church. Not many people weep uncontrollably throughout the services. After a few weeks, she got into a small group with some other women. Their love and support changed her life. Gradually, she began to rise out of the ashes of her broken, abusive marriage.

Sarah began to smile again, and she realized God was at work to restore her heart and her kids. She learned important lessons about God showing up in our time of pain. The Lord was healing her wounds. After a few months, the group leader saw a need for an apprentice leader, and she suggested Sarah. When the leader approached her, Sarah shook her head and almost laughed, "You've got to be kidding! I don't know the Bible very well at all. And besides, I have way too much on my plate. I'm a single mom trying to hold a job and raise two children. I don't have the time, energy, knowledge, or ability to help lead a group. No. Not me. Not now. No way!"

A day or two later, Sarah was praying, and the Holy Spirit changed her direction. She felt sure the Spirit was directing her to call her leader and accept the role of an apprentice. In spite of all her objections, God had a different plan. From the moment she said yes she began to experience a surge of God's favor that lifted her and her children to new heights. The Scriptures spoke more clearly to her heart, she sensed God's presence, she got a promotion at work so she had more income, and her children somehow realized she wasn't as dumb as they'd thought. They began to talk with her, treat her with respect, and obey without raising objections (not too many objections, anyway). Sarah's daughter saw her mother step out to serve God, and she became one of the leaders in her student ministry. Sarah's son got involved in a worship band.

Nothing in Sarah's family situation had changed—her husband was still in prison, he still said and did hurtful things, she was still living as a single mom, and she still had tons of responsibility at work and at home—but Sarah had changed. God was pouring out His blessings on her because she took a first step of faith.

A year later, Sarah's group leader moved to a different city, and Sarah became the new small group leader. She remarked, "I never dreamed that God would trust me to serve Him and these women. It's an incredible honor." It all began because she was willing to focus on something other

When she took Jesus' hand and stepped out to serve others, the heavens opened for her.

than her own problems. When she took Jesus' hand and stepped out to serve others, the heavens opened for her. Oh, Sarah had plenty of reasons to avoid taking these steps. She could have pointed to the emotional pain she was experiencing, the lack of time, the responsibilities of raising two children, and many other excuses. But after her initial reluctance, she refused to let those get in the way of humble submission and glad partnership. She was all in. Sarah's decision to live for something beyond herself helped to establish her children on the right path. Kids need to see that their parents have a vision for life that's beyond mere survival. They want to know their own lives count, and the best way for them to come to that conclusion is for them to see it in their parents—or at least in one of them. A clearer vision and a higher calling breathe life into everyone around, especially the children. They're sponges that soak up every attitude, value, and habit in their environment.

Priorities

When we think of priorities, we usually think of ordering our day and our week—and maybe our lives—so we focus on the important things, and we don't allow the urgent to crowd them out. We look at our schedules, budgets, and to-do lists. There is, however, a priority we often overlook.

God had asked me, "Have you considered that I have problems?" When I realized that God's problems were far more important than mine, He asked me a second question, "Will you put my problems first?"

Like most normal human beings, the prospect of putting God's agenda ahead of my own felt awkward and threatening. Starting with Adam and Eve in the Garden, submission to God hasn't exactly been strong in the human condition! Many questions swirled in my mind. What would I have to give up? How hard would it be? What would He ask of me? Could I possibly overcome my inherent selfishness to put God's agenda first in my life? I'd been a Christian for many years, and I had often talked about the need to be obedient to God . . . but this was different. This wasn't about isolated instances and choices. This was about the biggest, most global values of my life: Would I put God above all else, no matter what the cost?

Then, God gave me a promise. He reminded me of a familiar passage in the most famous message Jesus spoke. He told the crowd on the hillside, "But seek first his kingdom and his righteousness, and all these things will be given to you as well" (Matt. 6:33).

Living for a person or a cause other than one's self seems odd, maybe even wrong. To most of us, it just doesn't make sense. Most people have a "scarcity mentality," and we believe we're in a "zero sum game." We assume our needs and goals are the most important things in the world, and we have a limited amount of resources to meet those needs and achieve those goals. We conclude that it only makes sense to devote every ounce of energy, time, and money to make ourselves happy and successful and in control. This thinking, however, leaves us feeling like there's "never enough" to fulfill our desires.

A "kingdom mentality" is different. We're still aware of our needs, hopes, and dreams, but our finite, flawed resources don't limit us. When we put God's priorities first, He promises to unleash the resources of heaven into our lives. That's what happened to Sarah, and her story is one among countless others. God is a "more than enough" God. Our King has all the resources in heaven and earth, and He's waiting on us to put Him first.

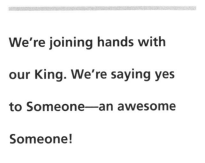

We're joining hands with our King. We're saying yes to Someone—an awesome Someone!

Jesus' invitation and promise aren't just a formula or a system we follow with guaranteed results. His plan is much richer (and more complicated) than that. We aren't following the directions to install and learn a software program so we can be more successful. We're joining hands with our King. We're saying yes to Someone—an awesome Someone! Far too many of us have had a business relationship with God. We've negotiated a deal with Him, swapping bits of obedience (attending church, cutting back on bad language, giving some money, and using many other "chips" in the game) for God's blessings. God, though, doesn't want to have a business relationship, and He doesn't want to play a game. He longs for us to respond to Him as our great and gracious King. That's what He deserves. Theologians talk about the nature of God as transcendent and imminent: He holds the vast expanse of all creation in the palm of His hand, but He tenderly cares for each of us and knows every hair on our heads (or that used to be on our heads). He exists in the farthest galaxy and is as close as our breath. He is supremely worthy of our affection, loyalty, and joyful obedience.

When Jesus gave us the promise to be "more than enough" if we put Him first, He wasn't oblivious to our fears and doubts. In fact, His promise comes in the context of identifying the normal reluctance to trust in God. The people listening to Him that day worried about the same things that consume our minds: making ends meet and paying the bills. But unlike us, most of them were extremely poor and lived under the domination of an occupying army. They were economically, socially, and politically oppressed. Most of the people in our country have no conception of this level of poverty (even "poor people" usually have a car and cable television), but I've seen it on trips overseas. A few years ago, I traveled to Rwanda where about a million people died in a genocidal civil war that began in 1994. The hotel where I stayed had a modest breakfast buffet, and each morning, I ate and enjoyed a couple cups of coffee. After a few days, I developed a relationship with one of the waiters. He was a thin man with a big smile. He told me his parents had died of disease, so he had moved from his village to the capitol city to find a job. I was there on July 4th, which happens to be Liberation Day in Rwanda. That day, I asked, "What are you going to do to celebrate today?"

He smiled and answered, "I've saved enough money, so I'm going to buy a cup of coffee!" Here he had been serving me coffee and a buffet of food every morning. He stood politely doing his job and serving my needs, yet he couldn't afford even one cup of the beverage he served me every day.

I walked away from this conversation with two overwhelming thoughts: tremendous gratitude for all God has given me and our family, but also a sharp, new awareness of the desperate needs in the lives of many hidden people.

The people Jesus addressed that day on the mountainside were much like the man in the hotel restaurant: poor and desperately needy. He didn't respond by telling them simply, "Don't worry." He pointed them to the compassionate heart and infinite resources of God as the antidote to worry. He told them this:

> "Therefore I tell you, do not worry about your life, what you will eat or drink; or about your body, what you will wear. Is not life more important than food, and the body more important than clothes? Look at the birds of the air; they do not sow or reap or store away in barns, and yet your heavenly Father feeds them. Are you not much more valuable than they? Who of you by worrying can add a single hour to his life? And why do you worry about clothes? See how the lilies of the field grow. They do not labor or spin. Yet I tell you that not even Solomon in all his splendor was dressed like one of these. If that is how God clothes the grass of the field, which is here

today and tomorrow is thrown into the fire, will he
not much more clothe you, O you of little faith? So
do not worry, saying, 'What shall we eat?' or 'What
shall we drink?' or 'What shall we wear?' For the pa-
gans run after all these things, and your heavenly
Father knows that you need them" (Matt. 6:25–32).

The people listening to Jesus needed food and clothes,
but Jesus told them to raise their sights to a higher priority. God cared about their immediate, physical needs, but
He cared even more about their hearts. The God of infinite
power and love has no problem providing for tangible needs.
But more than that, He wants our hearts.

Jesus told the poor people of Palestine to put Him and
His kingdom first, and He's telling the poor man in Rwanda
to put Him first. He's saying the same thing to you and me.
The problem for them was trusting that Jesus would come
through and provide for their basic needs. The problem for
many of us is that we aren't sure He'll give us all we want or
need. His promise, then, surfaces a crisis of faith. The inherent questions for all of us include: Is putting His kingdom
first worth it? Does He really care? Will He come through
like He promised?

If we wait until we have plenty of money, possessions,
and comfort before we put the King and His kingdom first,
we'll never get there. No matter how much we have, it will
never be enough. We'll keep raising the bar until we have
just a little bit more and a little bit more. No matter where
we are on the economic spectrum—from the richest to the
poorest—aligning our hearts with God's is the first step in
experiencing His blessings. Jesus gave us the Lord's Prayer to

point us to this alignment. We pray, "Your kingdom come, your will be done on earth as it is in heaven" (Matt. 6:10). One of the chief components of this prayer is to remind us that a right heart is aligned with God's. We submit our wills to Him, and we desire His purposes and His honor above all else. Why is this said in our most commonly used prayer? Because we need to be reminded so often!

To play it safe, some of us try to reduce the Christian life to a formula. However, those who see Christianity as a formula of obedience and blessing are often disappointed. When they give but God doesn't give back as much or as quickly as they expect, they feel He's let them down. Jesus offers a relationship, not a formula. We become generous because we've

We become generous because we've received so much from God that our hearts and resources overflow into the lives of others.

received so much from God that our hearts and resources overflow into the lives of others. There is no promise that we'll become financially rich because we give, but we can expect the fabulous riches of a "well done" response from the King and the joy of seeing lives changed. The real blessing isn't in receiving things, but in developing a deeper relationship with the King. That's enough. That's plenty. Look at what Jesus told the people that day: If the Father cares for birds and flowers, how much more does He care for you? God isn't "barely enough"; He's "far more than enough." When we grasp this fact, we'll unclench our fists, open our hearts, and put Him first in every aspect of our lives. Our relationship with the King is the foundation of our choice to make Him and His kingdom our highest priority. It makes perfect sense.

When we put God's kingdom first and give to others, we aren't giving out of a vacuum. We give out of the abundance of God's generosity to us. A sense of entitlement *demands more*, but a heart of gratitude longs to *give more* as a response to the wonder of God's love and resources poured out for us. Then, the cycle of extravagant generosity rolls on: We're overwhelmed with God's goodness, so we give out of grateful hearts; God then reciprocates by blessing us even more, which produces more gratitude and generosity, and on and on. But it's not about the things God gives—it's about the King who gives them.

God's promise is phenomenal, but it doesn't eliminate risks and heartaches. We're fallen people living in a fallen world, and the Bible tells us that we can expect difficulties. In fact, some of the hardships we face are the direct result of our grace-motivated obedience to Christ. Jesus warned that those who put Him first will be persecuted, and we aren't exempt from the normal struggles of life. Love for Jesus and loyalty to His cause give us the highest purpose in life, but they don't protect us from all harm. No one was ever as obedient to the Father as Jesus, and look what happened to Him. No believer was as committed to Christ as Paul, and his story is a litany of rejection and hardship—in addition to the joy of seeing lives changed.

God as Father

When Jesus told the people "your heavenly Father knows that you need them," His reference to God probably raised a few eyebrows. Throughout the Old Testament, God was most often seen as fierce and unapproachable. God led the people out of Egypt with pillars of fire and smoke. When Moses went up Mount Sinai and the mountain shook, the people were terrified at God's awesome power and presence. In a few places, the prophets talked about God's tenderness, but more often, they warned of His fierce judgment. In the Sermon on the Mount and throughout His life, Jesus spoke of God in terms that were unfamiliar to those who were listening. Could God really be affectionate, protective, supportive, and present like a Jewish dad with his beloved kids? Earlier in this sermon, Jesus had told them to pray, "Our Father in heaven" (Matt. 6:9). To the Jews in the first century, this was a revolutionary way to think about relating to God. It still is for us in the twenty-first century. And after He gave the promise about pouring out His blessings if we put Him first, Jesus again painted a picture of how God longs to relate to us as a loving Father. He told them, "Which of you, if his son asks for bread, will give him a stone? Or if he asks for a fish, will give him a snake? If you, then, though you are evil, know how to give good gifts to your children, how much more will your Father in heaven give good gifts to those who ask him!" (Matt. 7:9–11)

This kind of relationship with God radically changes us. Sometimes, people come up to me and say, "Your son looks a lot like you." But one of the biggest compliments I receive is when someone says, "Your son acts like you!" (Come to think of it, that truth can be kind of frightening— for both of us.) When we put God's agenda first, something

> **When we put God's agenda first, something more than our schedule changes. God begins to change us from the inside out.**

more than our schedule changes. God begins to change us from the inside out. We don't just tack on right behaviors because we're supposed to. We start taking on the family likeness. Just as a loved boy copies his dad and a loved girl wants to dress and act like her mom, we start thinking, feeling, and acting more like God, our Father.

If we spend our time focusing on our problems and our expectations, we may get some answers, but it will never feel like enough. No matter how much we get, we'll always want more, and we'll never be completely satisfied. But if we change agendas and put the King first, we get far more than additional resources (as wonderful as that is)—we get the King, and He fills us with more peace, purpose, and power than we ever dreamed we could enjoy. Like beloved children, we begin to take on His nature. We'll want the things He wants; we'll love the people He loves.

In one of David's familiar psalms, he listed many benefits of forgiveness, healing, and rescue from sin and hell. Then he wrote that God "crowns you with love and compassion" (Ps. 103:4). When I thought about that phrase, I realized that only royalty wears a crown. When God forgave us, He didn't make us slaves. He adopted us as His children, so we became princes and princesses in His kingdom! And what is the crown we wear? His love and compassion. That's what people see when we put the King first. They can tell—and we can tell—that we're children of the King when these traits become evident in our lives. As His children, we're heirs who will inherit incredible blessings someday in the new heaven and new earth. All of that awaits us, but even now, we have the privilege of representing the King every moment of every day.

Some of us easily understand Jesus' assurance that we have a loving heavenly Father. I'm one of those people. My father is a wonderful example of love and strength. I have never doubted his integrity, affection, or interest in me. When I talk about my mother and father, people often say, "Wow, that's fantastic! To be honest, I'm really jealous!" Many people, however, have strained or broken relationships with their dads—and some fathers have abandoned their kids. These people can't *compare* God to their dads; they have to draw a *contrast* between them. They can say, "My father was harsh (or distant or manipulative or whatever), but God is attentive, loving, and active in my life." No matter what our family backgrounds may be, everyone has an image of the ideal father. Those who have a "father deficit" have to work harder and dig deeper to grasp the nature of God as our Father, but when they get there, they appreciate Him so much. The Bible says that God has adopted us as His children. Professor J. I. Packer says that the language of the New Testament indicates that we aren't second-class kids in God's family. He loves us just as much as Jesus. Packer describes the wonder of this truth:

> God receives us as sons [and daughters], and loves us with the same steadfast affection with which He eternally loves His beloved only-begotten. There are no distinctions of affection in the divine family. We are all loved just as fully as Jesus is loved. It is like a fairy story—the reigning monarch adopts waifs and strays to make princes of them—but, praise God, it is not a fairy story: it is hard and solid fact, founded on the bedrock of free and sovereign grace. This, and nothing less than this, is what adoption means. No

wonder that John cries, "Behold, what manner of love . . . !" When once you understand adoption, your heart will cry the same.[8]

I've talked to men and women who don't believe God is a loving Father, so they excuse themselves from putting His kingdom first. I understand their reluctance, but I've noticed that these people seldom get over the hump in their spiritual lives. They stay stuck. They've been waiting on God, but God is waiting on them to take His hand and trust Him to lead them to a deeper relationship. If they find the courage to trust the Bible's clear description of God's affection as our Father—no matter how tentative the first step may be—they turn a key that unlocks their hearts and lets the love of God flood in. It may not happen soon, and it certainly won't happen instantly, but it will happen. It's not my promise; it's God's.

> **If they find the courage to trust the Bible's clear description of God's affection as our Father—no matter how tentative the first step may be—they turn a key that unlocks their hearts and lets the love of God flood in.**

Actually, people often come to God with a list of preconditions before they're willing to put Him first. Some have experienced deep emotional wounds, and they insist that God heal them before they value Him above all else. Others cling to the hope of promotion or wealth, or they say they're trying to get their lives completely in order before they're ready to make the plunge. All of these are smokescreens for selfishness and fear. They don't want to submit to God, so they come up with any excuse that sounds plausible at the time, but in their hearts, they don't trust that God will fill the emptiness. They think the risk is too great and He won't come through.

Jesus asks us to think, look around, and realize God is already fulfilling His promise to the birds and flowers. Surely, surely, Jesus will fulfill it for us, too. After all, He loves us so much He died to prove Himself to us. Paul echoes this perspective in his letter to the Romans. He asked, "If God didn't hesitate to put everything on the line for us, embracing our condition and exposing himself to the worst by sending his own Son, is there anything else he wouldn't gladly and freely do for us?" (Rom. 8:32 *Message*)

A Key Question

As a helpful form of self-evaluation when I face choices, I often ask myself a question: "Lord, what would please you right now?"

In difficult, confusing situations, we often have dozens of conflicting thoughts, hopes, and fears. It's hard to sort them all out. We can begin to clear away the fog by asking God what would please Him. When we get in touch with His heart, at least some of the choices drop away. For instance, we know we can't lash out in anger, and He doesn't want us to lie to get out of a jam. Beyond that, I've learned to ask God to give me a clear mind so I can determine *the next right thing*. The situation may be incredibly complicated, so it's helpful to know my next step. In every relationship, every struggle, every opportunity, and every decision about finances, work, friendship, marriage, and parenting, I ask

God to show me the very next step that would please Him. It may be small or it could be huge, but it's only one step— the next one. We often think that aligning ourselves around God's kingdom is an enormous, global thing. In a way, it's the biggest decision we ever make (and we make it over and over again), but we live out our new kingdom values by taking one step at a time.

The next step often involves something we dread: death. But if we want to follow Jesus, we follow Him all the way to the cross. Jesus didn't try to soften His words when He told His disciples this concept:

> "If anyone would come after me, he must deny himself and take up his cross and follow me. For whoever wants to save his life will lose it, but whoever loses his life for me will find it. What good will it be for a man if he gains the whole world, yet forfeits his soul? Or what can a man give in exchange for his soul?" (Matt. 16:24–26)

Similarly, Paul described the Christian life this way: "We always carry around in our body the death of Jesus, so that the life of Jesus may also be revealed in our body. For we who are alive are always being given over to death for Jesus' sake, so that his life may be revealed in our mortal body" (2 Cor. 4:10–11). The part that needs to die is our selfishness and our rebellion against God's rule in our lives. That's probably the very thing that's been blocking the flow of the Spirit in us. It's the problem that throws us out of alignment with God's will.

When we're bold to ask the question about what pleases God, we're on the right track. If we weren't willing to ask the question, we'd stay stuck in the past. When we ask, we're at least beginning to pursue God, His will, and His ways. And then, we need to listen. The Spirit delights for us to open our hearts to Him. He'll show us anything that displeases Him so we can take it to the cross, confess it, and experience God's cleansing forgiveness and love.

Recently, I shared these thoughts in one of my weekend messages at Allison Park Church. An elderly couple in the audience had been experiencing increasing marital strife. The woman in the relationship was so frustrated with her husband that she had determined to leave him that same week. When the wife heard me teach about taking the next right step, she was furious. She wanted to leave her husband, but she knew it wouldn't please the Lord. She prayed and wrestled with God. Finally, she repented and found the courage to go home and tell her husband how much she loved him. He was shocked. They had been drifting apart for years, but soon, the fresh warmth of her love rekindled something in him. He began treating her with respect and then with genuine affection. After a few months had passed, she told me, "When I first heard you talk about taking the next right step, I hated you!" She laughed, so I knew this story had a good ending. She then said, "After I went home with a new commitment to my husband, something happened. I'm not sure what it was, but he changed! Today, we're more in love than we were when we got married. Before, I lived in constant turmoil, and I had no peace. Now, God has given me His peace. Our marriage isn't perfect—because I'm still part of it! But God has transformed my husband, me, and our relationship. Pastor, thank you so much!"

> **Confessing our sins to one another can be one of the hardest things we ever do, but it results in incredible freedom.**

Confessing our sins to one another can be one of the hardest things we ever do, but it results in incredible freedom. When I spoke at our church on doing the next right thing, I shared a passage in James about confessing our sins to one another. A young man contacted me and said, "Pastor, I need to tell you something. I'm addicted to pornography, and I need help." In the process of admitting his problem, confessing his sin, and seeking assistance, this young man got his life back. By his admission, porn had consumed his money, his time, his relationships, his mind, and his heart. Doing the next right thing brought a freedom he had forgotten even existed.

Phil, an engineer, is a leader in our church. He worked for the same company since graduating from college twenty years earlier. When his company merged with a competitor, another man in his department received a promotion instead of him. Feeling bypassed was hard, but it was only the beginning of Phil's trouble. The new boss had been jealous of Phil for a long time, and when he became his supervisor, he made up an excuse to let him go. Suddenly, Phil wasn't only without a promotion; he was out of a job. He was certainly hurt and frustrated, but he made a commitment to God to avoid vengeful words against the man who fired him. I watched Phil walk through this difficult season. Every day, he made a commitment to do the next right thing to please God. He held his tongue, and he chose to give thanks and trust God for his future. He continued to give generously even though his funds were being depleted. After about two months, something happened at the company. He got a call one day, asking him to come back and take his previous position. The man who fired him had been dismissed, and Phil was reinstated with a nice raise. Some people might say all that was a coincidence, and it would have happened even if Phil hadn't trusted God in the valley of emotional, financial, and vocational upheaval. Phil doesn't buy it. He's convinced that God poured out His blessings because he chose to put God's kingdom first.

When I ask the question, "Lord, what pleases you?" I'm inviting God to rule over my attitude and my actions. Considering this question enables me to reorient my heart to be aligned with God's purposes. This process shapes my internal perspective. Then, I can ask the questions we addressed in the previous chapter: "God, what's your problem? What's on your heart?" These take my attention off myself and shift it outside. I look for difficulties in other people's lives, occasionally global, but often local and immediate. God brings people to mind. I might think of a man who recently lost his wife to a long illness. I can call him and offer friendship and support. The Lord might remind me of a friend who is going through a hard time. I can take a few minutes and send an email to show I'm thinking of him. Sometimes, God reminds me about a huge problem in the world, like human trafficking, AIDS

> **When I ask the question, "Lord, what pleases you?" I'm inviting God to rule over my attitude and my actions.**

orphans, homelessness, refugees, dirty water, or political prisoners. I can spend some time praying for organizations that are equipped to help, or I may marshal some resources in our family or in our church. Quite often, God shows me needs in people's lives that I would have missed if I hadn't gone through the process of first reorienting my heart and then looking for others' problems.

The order of these two questions, though, can sometimes be reversed. Harold McKamish owns a large sheet metal company in Pittsburgh. About twenty years ago, Harold moved to Phoenix, Arizona, to open a branch of his company. Harold and his wife, Daisy, found a church to attend. One Sunday morning during the service, Harold felt God was directing him to give some money to one of the men in the church. At first, he questioned his impression. He didn't know the man and had no information about him. However, after some turmoil in his spirit, he decided to follow the impression.

During the following week, the man, Brother Nel, called Harold and asked if they could meet. When they talked, Harold discovered he was a retired pastor who had very little food in his home. Brother Nel was struggling financially because he often traveled to Mexico and gave his money to help the people there. Brother Nel invited Harold to go with him to San Luis, Mexico. His heart for the plight of the Mexican people deeply touched Harold.

Time after time, Harold asked God to give him direction for the next right thing. He instantly knew he had gotten in touch with God's problem, and he felt compelled to do something to alleviate the suffering in the city. He began to formulate a plan and take steps to help the children and people in San Luis. Over the years, he launched a ministry called Caring Hearts, which has now built an orphanage with a school, a church, a home for teenage boys, a center for the blind, and a soup kitchen to provide food to feed many malnourished children and adults.

Harold is a man with great personal resources, and he has invested much of his wealth in this effort. But he didn't do it all alone. As others found out what God was doing through him, he became a funnel for funds, medical and dental professionals, manpower, and material to flow into the work. God's problem stuck in Harold's heart, and he then intuitively asked, "Lord, what is the next right thing for me to do to help these people?" God has used Harold to radically change countless lives—poor people in Mexico who now have a higher standard of living and a new sense of hope, and people in America who have gotten involved to be partners with God and with Harold to care for "the least of these." It's a good match.

Simple Obedience

Some people assume that reorienting our lives to put the King and His kingdom first is always a dramatic event. Sometimes, it is. When Jesus appeared to Paul on the road to Damascus, Paul's direction in life took a 180-degree turn! He had been on a mission to capture and kill Christians, but suddenly he was on a mission to lead people to Christ. It doesn't get any more dramatic than that. For most of us, however, the shift doesn't come with blinding lights, but with directional signals. We sense God's Spirit blinking in our hearts, and we finally pay attention. We may have questions, fears, and doubts, but sooner or later, we take the first right step to embrace the King and His kingdom. Then we take the next, and the next, and the next. Each time, we face our fears and make the choice.

In Matthew's gospel, Jesus went to the Jordan River to be baptized by John the Baptist. Why did He go? He told John it was "to fulfill all righteousness"—in other words, to do the next right thing. As soon as He took that step of obedience, the heavens opened and the Father announced, "This is my Son, whom I love; with him I am well pleased" (Matt. 3:17).

The pattern is the same in our lives. When we say, "God, I want to please you by doing the next thing you want me to do," the heavens open up and we sense God's pleasure.

When we say, "God, I want to please you by doing the next thing you want me to do," the heavens open up and we sense God's pleasure.

Most often, it's not an audible voice like Jesus, John, and the others heard that day on the banks of the Jordan. It's the still, small voice of the Spirit, whispering to our hearts, "Way to go! I'm so pleased with you!"

But that's not the end of the story. It's just the beginning. The next verse says, "Then Jesus was led by the Spirit into the desert" (Matt. 4:1). The Spirit led Jesus into the next thing the Father wanted Him to do.

Simple obedience puts us in line with the pleasure of God and the purpose of God. Not long ago, I heard a talk by Andy Stanley, a pastor in the Atlanta area. One of his points was that the Holy Spirit often communicates with us in what seems like a friend or spouse clearing his throat to get our attention, "Ughmmm." It's not loud, it's not dramatic, and it's not very clear—at least at first. When we notice, we stop and think, *What's going on? What am I missing?* Stanley suggested that many of us may have heard the Spirit "clear His throat" as He talked about sin, confession, and our hearts aligning with God. When Melodie does that to me, I immediately know I need to pay attention. I'm missing something important! Sometimes, I look at her, and she'll nod or grimace or give me some idea of what she's thinking.

As you read this chapter, have you heard the Spirit "clear His throat"? When we looked at the promise of Matthew 6:33, did your heart skip a beat? Did you feel fear or hope? Both are signs that you're getting it! When we asked the question about pleasing God, did it prick your conscience and compel you to make something right? When we looked again at uncovering God's problem, did you remember a troubled friend you need to call? I hope so. That's what this chapter is all about. It happens to me all the time when I look at these passages and ask these questions. The King is rarely ambiguous about what He wants us to do next.

Some people try to get out of all this by insisting, "I don't even know where to begin. It's too big, too confusing, and too hard." That's not the case. We begin by listening to the Spirit and responding in simple obedience. The next right thing is often to confess a bad attitude, ask someone for forgiveness, tell the truth, give something back, stop complaining and help with housework, or make a phone call to help a friend. Quite often, we complain about God not giving us a clear direction when we haven't obeyed the directions He's already given.

I can honestly say that I've never heard anyone say he regretted obeying God. It's sometimes hard, but it's always worth it. The people who refuse to obey, though, often are plagued with regrets.

Alignment with the King begins with a single step of obedience. Before we obey, we often experience fear of the unknown. When we've seen God come through a few times, however, we realize the King may be mysterious, but He's supremely trustworthy.

Consider This

1. What are some reasons people resist submitting to God and His will? What do they fear?

2. How does it affect us to see God as "never enough"? How does it affect us to see Him as "more than enough"?

3. How would you describe the promise in Matthew 6:33? What does it (or would it) mean in your life to "seek first His kingdom and His righteousness"?

4. When you try to relate to God as a loving Father, can you compare your earthly father to Him favorably, or do you have to make contrasts? Where are you in your pursuit of seeing yourself as God's beloved child?

5. What impact does (or can) the question, "God, what pleases you?" have on your heart and your direction?

6. How does the question about pleasing God fit with the one about identifying God's problem? Which seems to come first? Explain your answer.

7. What's the next right step for you? When and how are you going to do it?

chapter 5

The Power of Delight

My deepest awareness of myself is that I am deeply loved by Jesus Christ and I have done nothing to earn it or deserve it.

Brennan Manning

The Bible describes two different ways of trying to relate to God. We find these throughout the pages of Scripture. Two people may do exactly the same spiritual activities but with diametrically different motivations. One reads the Bible, prays, goes to church, gives to charities, and serves out of a heart overflowing with gratitude for the incredible grace of God. Another person does exactly the same activities, but to impress God (and others) and gain leverage with Him. This one may never say it, and he may not even think it clearly, but his responses to difficulties show he believes that God is somehow indebted to him because of all his efforts to earn the right to be blessed.

In the story we usually call "The Prodigal Son," the younger son returned home after wasting his inheritance on a wild lifestyle. His father, representing God, saw him from a distance and ran to him, interrupted his confession, hugged and kissed him, and threw a huge party to celebrate. It's a picture of God's extravagant love and forgiveness. But there's another son in the story, the elder brother. When his wayward brother came home, he was out in the field, hard at work. When he learned his father was throwing an expensive party because his little brother had come home, the elder son was furious. He felt superior because he had been so faithful to work so hard while his younger brother had been unfaithful and unworthy of his father hosting a celebration. He deeply resented his father's kindness to his brother and felt no joy in his younger brother's return. Both sons had wanted their father's things more than their father, but only one (the unlikely one) had come to his senses and found the love he'd always wanted. The story ends with the father pleading with his elder son to come in and join the feast. One son recognized his need for repentance and forgiveness, but the other didn't.

Jesus told parables about the difference between self-righteous Pharisees who did all the right things for the wrong reasons, and humble, repentant, grateful sinners who experienced the grace of God. We've looked at several passages from Jesus' Sermon on the Mount. One of the most striking passages explains the contrast Jesus draws between righteousness and unrighteousness. We normally think of "good people" who are committed to religious and moral choices, and we contrast them with those who are blatant, evil sinners. That's not the contrast Jesus draws at all. He paints a picture of two people who give, two people who pray, and two people who fast—one does these things to be noticed and applauded by other people, while the other does them for the pure delight of knowing and pleasing God.

Self-justification is the default mode of the human heart. We naturally want to perform to earn points with God and win the acclamation of others. It seems completely normal, but it's poison to our spiritual lives. I know. I've been there.

Light in the Darkness

I grew up in a wonderful family. My mom and dad were—and are—the most loving and supportive parents I've ever seen. When I was growing up, I had every advantage of being pointed to the grace of God. By the time I graduated from Bible college, I was the poster child for a pastor's son. I was the senior class president. I'd never smoked, drunk alcohol, or used drugs, and I had been sexually pure. I talked often about the wonderful grace of God, but somewhere in the depths of my heart, I believed I was one of God's prize kids because I'd made so many right choices. I was pretty sure God felt lucky to have me on His team because I was so committed to Him and His kingdom.

After graduation, I was at my parents' home one night. I was fasting and praying, and I told God, "Lord, I want you to know that if everyone else stops trusting you and serving you, I'll stay faithful. You can always count on me."

A few weeks later, I was going to seminary and living in one of the dorms as a dean of students on the hall. Late one night, I was reading Luke 22. My eyes fell on the conversation between Jesus and Peter near the end of the Last Supper. Jesus was about to be betrayed, arrested, tried, convicted, tortured, and killed. Peter assured Him, "Lord, I am ready to go with you to prison and to death" (Luke 22:33). Peter went on to compare himself to the other disciples, "Even if all these others forsake you, you can count on me. I'm different from them. I am truly loyal and committed to you."

Peter's words were, I instantly realized, eerily like the ones I'd prayed only weeks before.

Jesus had a startling announcement for Peter. He called him by his given name—the way parents use their child's full name when they say something serious. Jesus told him, "Simon, Simon, Satan has asked to sift you as wheat. But I have prayed for you, Simon, that your faith may not fail. And when you have turned back, strengthen your brothers" (Luke 22:31–32).

I sensed the Holy Spirit say to me, "Jeff, this passage is for you."

When I'm reading the Scriptures and the Lord whispers that a verse is for me, I'm usually encouraged. This time, I felt devastated. This was not the word I wanted to hear. I would have preferred, "God is going to bless you abundantly," or "You are getting ready to inherit a lot of money." Instead, God was saying to me, "Jeff, Satan is going to sift you like wheat." What could that possibly mean?

> **When I'm reading the Scriptures and the Lord whispers that a verse is for me, I'm usually encouraged. This time, I felt devastated.**

About five minutes later, my phone rang. It was my mother. For the first and only time in my life, she said, "Jeff, I was just praying for you, and the Lord brought a verse to mind. I think He wants me to share it with you."

I didn't want to ask, but I did anyway, "What is it, Mom?"

She read the verses from Luke 22 that I'd just read. Maybe, I could have blown off the Holy Spirit's whisper to me a few minutes earlier as the effect of dorm food, but I couldn't deny God's clear voice in my mother's phone call.

That night, a season of sifting began in my life. For eighteen months, I lived with constant anxiety and fear. I guess you could say that I began to question everything about my life—which produced a state of constant anxiety. I questioned my salvation, and I wondered if God could ever use me again. Before that night, I had thought all the time about my successes and accolades, but suddenly, images of past failures haunted my mind. Sins I'd buried long ago came to the surface, and I experienced gnawing guilt. Melodie and I were dating, and I worried about what it meant to be open and vulnerable to someone—even someone who showed every sign of trusting and loving me. I was filled with so much guilt, fear, and anxiety that I had difficulty making it through each day. Until that time, I'd never even come close to a panic attack, but now, panic was my constant experience. All day, every day, the minutes seemed like hours, and the hours seemed like months. It was all I could do to keep going. My confidence, which was once so strong, had been shattered. This season of my life was a spiritual shakedown, and I had no idea it would ever end.

After a year and a half, I was in the shower one day, and I cried out, "God, you've got to help me! I'm going out of my mind! I don't know what to do. Please, help me!"

As I prayed, a verse of Scripture came to mind. I don't remember ever memorizing it, but God had implanted it in the recesses of my thinking some time before. Now, it was time for Him to bring it to the surface. The verse is found in several places in the Bible. One of them is in Romans. Paul had been explaining the power of the gospel to trans-form lives, and then he wrote, "Anyone who trusts in him will never be put to shame" (Rom. 10:11). Instantly, it felt like God had let a rope down into the pit of despair where I'd been living for the past year and a half. For the next few weeks, I quoted this verse hundreds of times every day. It was light and salt, life and breath to me. As I quoted it, I let it sink deep into my heart. I thought about each word and the message God wanted to speak to me. I realized He was saying, "Jeff, don't trust yourself because you'll never have enough, do enough, or be enough. Trust only in me. If you trust in yourself, you'll feel anxious, afraid, and full of guilt. But if you trust in me, I'll never let you be put to shame. You can count on me, but count *only* on me."

In those long, devastating months, all of my pride, my confidence in my performance, and my ability to win the approval of others had been crushed by the realization that I wasn't what I thought I was. Now, at the bottom of the pit of despair, God overwhelmed me with a new realization of His grace. I have nothing—nothing—to offer God. If He accepts me, it's only because of His grace. If He leads me, it's only because of His grace. If He uses me, it's only because of His grace. I'd intellectually known the truth about grace before, but now, I was experiencing it in the depths of my soul. I still had to choose to obey, but for a very different reason. I had obeyed to earn points, to prove myself to God, and to win the approval of those who were watching. I changed and be-gan to choose to obey simply because I want my life to honor the one who loves me, bought me, and accepts me in spite of all my faults and flaws.

We can obey out of duty or delight, and the two are poles apart. When our motivation is gratitude and love, everything changes. Paul described it this way: "For Christ's love compels us, because we are convinced that one died for all, and therefore all died. And he died for all, that those who live should no longer live for themselves but for him who died for them and was raised again" (2 Cor. 5:14-15). My obedience doesn't earn anything, but it accomplishes something much better: It connects me with the heart of God because I'm saying yes to Him each time I choose to obey.

Repeating the Class

When I mentioned that self-justification is the default mode of the human heart, I didn't imply that it vanishes when we trust in Christ. We need to be reminded of God's grace, again and again. It's easy to forget . . . too easy.

After I'd been a pastor for about ten years and had planted five more churches, I was grateful for the opportunity to be God's partner in this work, but the pressures of life and work began to crowd out the sense of God's delight. We had been involved in building a new facility, developing leadership, and experiencing normal family stresses. One Saturday, I was in my office preparing for my Sunday message, and I had a skull-splitting migraine. I'd never had one before, but I'd heard enough people describe them to know what it was. I fell to the floor and crawled to the bathroom where I could lie on the cool tile floor in the pitch-black darkness. My vision was blurred, I was nauseated, and bright light felt like a dagger thrust into my head. After two hours, I finally called Melodie and asked her to come get me. The debilitating pain lasted three weeks. During this time, I lay perfectly still on a bed in a room with the curtains pulled, and I had a bandana over my eyes to block out any ray of light. I had plenty of time to think and pray, and I asked, "Lord, what in the world is going on? What are you trying to say to me?"

At some point during those weeks, I realized my headache was more than a physical problem. I was suffering from physical, emotional, and spiritual burnout. When the headaches subsided to a tolerable level, I made an appointment with a counselor. After only a couple of sessions, he gave me the results of an emotional health assessment he'd given me. As he held the report in his hands, I could see a graph with a spike at one point. He said, "Jeff, the spike on the graph indicates that you have a very serious fear of failure. You're driving yourself in an unhealthy way because you're terrified of failing."

I was afraid of failure—and even the threat of failure—because I interpreted failure as a devastating blow to my security.

I wanted to argue with him. Afraid of failing? That can't be right. After all, I was a risk-taker. I was willing to confront the hard issues. I was leading people through change. How could I be afraid of failing if I was willing to take these risks in leadership?

My counselor anticipated my resistance and questions. He explained that even my success was creating a fear of failure. It was all about motivation: I was afraid of failure—and even the threat of failure—because I interpreted failure as a devastating blow to my security.

He asked, "Jeff, if you fail, will God love you any less?"

I wanted to say, "Look! I'm a pastor. I know the right answer," but I just shook my head, no.

He then asked a harder question: "If it's God's will for you to fail for a season—not morally or ethically, but fail in terms of your achievements, and your failure would eventually bring Him more glory, would you be willing to fail?" To make sure I understood, he restated his question: "If failure would bring God more glory than success, would you be okay with that?"

I smiled weakly and told him, "I know the right answer, but I assume you want me to be honest."

He nodded knowingly. I then said, "No. Actually, I'm not okay with failure."

As we talked, I realized I'd forgotten the lessons I'd learned years before, and I'd wrapped my identity around my success and the applause of others—again. This time, I didn't have to go through agony for eighteen months to find an answer. I'd been in this class before. I knew the curriculum—and even more, I knew the heart of the Teacher.

Success had become an idol. I loved the power success brought, but the dark side of this thirst was the fear of being humiliated by failure. I enjoyed the affirmation of people who participated in the success, but I couldn't handle the increased demands of never disappointing them. I had to learn again that God's affection for me isn't based on my success. His joy at being my Father doesn't hinge on my performance. He loves me, period. To drive the power of grace deeper into my daily life, I developed a set of confessions to retrain my thoughts. I prayed some of them early in the morning, and I made a point of praying others during the day. Here are the statements the Spirit and I used to retrain my mind:

- Lord, I know you love and accept me today by your grace, no matter whether I succeed or fail. (Eph. 2:8-10)

- Today, I will not just survive; I will overcome and conquer by your grace. (Rom. 8:37)

- Because of Christ, God has chosen to love me and accept me, and there's nothing I can do about it. I can't do anything to increase His acceptance, and I can't do anything to diminish it. It's His decision, and He's not going to change it. (Rom. 8:38-39)

- I can do all things through Christ who gives me strength. (Phil. 4:13)

- God's grace is sufficient for me, which means that there's more than enough, no matter what I face. (2 Cor. 12:7-10)

- Through the cross, I'm forgiven. That's a fact whether I feel forgiven or not. (1 John 1:9)

- Those who put their trust in Him will never, ever be put to permanent shame and dismayed by failure, for God is a God who redeems my life. (Rom. 10:11)

- Today, I choose to live in joy and not in dread because I know that if God is for me, then nothing can stand against me. (Rom. 8:31)

These statements aren't magic; they're reminders. Again and again, they reframed my thinking and pointed my heart back to the wonder of God, who lavishes His grace on us. I still need these reminders. I need them a lot.

Two Kinds of Poison

Self-justification—thinking we can earn our acceptance with God and approval from others—is certainly a poison, but there are two distinct kinds. *Pride* fills those who believe they're good enough, and intense *shame* fills those who realize they've failed to earn enough points. Both are based on the same premise that God bases His love and acceptance on our performance. Our identity, value, and future are tied up in our ability to succeed and please people—it's nothing less than idolatry.

One of the most important principles I've learned through my struggles to grasp God's grace is that genuine love is always a choice. People choose to love us, or they choose not to love us. It's a decision, not a feeling. Here's the radical life-changing truth about our Creator: He has already decided to love us. He loves you despite your past. He loves you regardless of your weakness. He demonstrated His love for you by being willing to go to the cross and suffer a horrific death to pay the price for your sin. He has made up His mind: He loves you. He loves you. He loves you—*and there's nothing you can do about it.*

Only when we recognize this fact are we able to experience true security and significance in our lives. Insecurity is the result of building our lives on anything that can be taken away, including our greatest strengths and talents, our accomplishments, our money, our status, our popularity, and the acceptance of those most important to us. The harsh reality is that any of those things can be taken away from us at any moment. If we build our sense of self on anything that's temporary, we've built our identity on shaky ground. We're only secure when we build our lives on the solid rock of God's unending love, forgiveness, and acceptance.

Security is the result of building our lives on a foundation that can never be taken away. There's only one thing in life that can never be taken away. What's that? It's God's choice to love us. We are secure only when we build our lives on that fact.

How do we know if we are truly secure and that our foundation is built properly? It's easy. How do we respond when we experience failure? When we're overlooked? When we're criticized? Certainly, we're not robots. These things hurt even the most secure people, but there's a big difference between being hurt and being devastated. If these losses crush us, we're putting too much stock in them.

Many passages of Scripture speak about idolatry and insecurity, as well as God's grace and love. Many people consider Paul's letter to the Romans to be one of the highlights of Scripture, and the eighth chapter is the pinnacle of the letter. He begins the chapter with the assurance that in Christ there is "no condemnation," and he ends with the promise of "no separation" from God's love no matter what we experience. A firm foundation of security is built on these truths.

Making It Real

At our church, we periodically hold weekend workshops during what we call a Spiritual Breakthrough Weekend. One of the most important issues in every person's life is the poison of building one's identity on personal performance. To help make the grace of God real, I teach about the foundation of God's choice to love, forgive, and accept us, and then I ask people to pray, "God, thank you that you have chosen to love and forgive me by your grace. I now choose to forgive myself. I release myself to step into the future you have for me."

Alicia had been a leader in various ministries of our church for years. When she attended a weekend workshop and was confronted with this prayer in the last session, her heart froze. She simply couldn't pray it.

As I led the group, I sensed something wasn't right. I stopped the workshop and said, "I feel like we haven't broken through yet, so I'm going to pray the prayer again. It seems there is somebody in the room who is having a problem with it, so we're going to pray again. Whoever you are, you need to say this out loud with the rest of us."

Alicia found the courage to speak the words of this prayer. She later told me, "Pastor, it was like a ton of weight was lifted off my shoulders! I finally felt forgiven. For years, I knew the truth about God's forgiveness and unconditional love, but this was the first moment I truly felt it. It's made all the difference!"

That day, something incredible happened to Alicia. Her fear, shame, and self-doubts were drowned in the endless sea of God's affection. She was no longer preoccupied with striving for success to prove herself or hiding her failures to protect her reputation. She felt free, but she also felt tremendously motivated. God's delight in her triggered a profound delight in Him. She gladly put Him first in her life and reoriented her priorities around His kingdom. She began to live to please the One who loves her so much, and she started asking, "God, what's your problem?" When she

> **That day, something incredible happened to Alicia. Her fear, shame, and self-doubts were drowned in the endless sea of God's affection.**

wasn't thinking about herself so much, she noticed many needs in the lives of people around her. To be honest, she had seen those needs before but had secretly resented the fact that she felt unworthy to meet them. Now, the despair was gone! She was filled up with Christ, and His love overflowed to heal hurts and meet needs in others' lives. She has become a magnet for hurting women. They can tell she has experienced deep wounds, but she's let God heal her. That's so attractive, so powerful. She doesn't smother them with love, and she doesn't demand compliance with her advice. Like Jesus, she offers love, forgiveness, and strength, and she lets people decide how to respond. Her compassion melts hearts, and the power of grace transforms lives.

Puritan pastor Jonathan Edwards understood the overwhelming nature of truly knowing God's love. His sermons were full of vivid descriptions of a heart delighting in God, such as the following:

> The enjoyment of God is the only happiness with which our souls can be satisfied. To go to heaven, fully to enjoy God, is infinitely better than the most pleasant accommodations here. Fathers and mothers, husbands, wives or children, or the company of earthly friends, are but shadows; but God is the substance. These are but scattered beams, but God is the sun. These are but streams. But God is the ocean.[9]

Before grace captures their hearts, people like Alicia feel like they don't belong in the Kingdom. In their minds, they've failed too badly or sinned too often. God surely can't accept them. But this assumption is based solely on the shifting sand of poor performance. These people are resistant to grace out of fear and shame, but when they finally understand, they're often shot out of a cannon to care for other hurting people.

On the other hand, modern-day Pharisees (and I confess that I used to be one of them) assume they're in the kingdom because they've jumped through all the hoops, avoided gross sins, and earned plenty of points with church activities. They're in just as much bondage as those who suffer from shame, but like the Pharisees in Jesus' day, they seldom realize it. They're super religious, but they're not free. They're always looking over their shoulder to see if anyone is doing more giving, praying, fasting, or serving. They're always measuring their performance against their own standards or someone else's, and they live with the nagging fear that all their efforts may not be enough. Of course, they never admit those doubts to anyone. That would make them appear vulnerable and weak—which is a fate worse than death for people who have built their identity on performing well! The only ones who are truly free to live a kingdom life, be honest about their flaws, and let the love of God overflow from them are those who are convinced—in the depths of their hearts—that it's all about grace, not about their performance.

Unfortunately, our innate penchant for performance is so strong that we often have to experience colossal failure or piercing heartache to come to the end of ourselves. When this happens, it's not an accident. It's God's gracious process to wake us up, make us come to our senses, and realize we've been all wrong. It often hurts so badly that we call it being "broken." That's how it feels, and that's what it actually is. God breaks our shell of wrong assumptions, empty lies, and false modesty. It hurts like crazy, but it's absolutely necessary.

That's what happened to me in seminary when I thought I was indispensable to God and again when my fear of failure drove me to emotional, physical, and spiritual burnout. When God brings us to the breaking point, it's not because He hates us. It's because He loves His children so much that He'll do anything to win our hearts back to Him.

Let me ask you a few questions:

- Have you recognized the games people play in their efforts to use performance to earn approval or hide failure?

- Have you seen how pride and shame about performance poison every thought, action, and relationship?

- Has God ever brought you to a point of brokenness? What happened? How did you respond?

- Will you pray, "God, thank you that you have chosen to love and forgive me by your grace; I now choose to forgive myself, and I release myself to step into the future you have for me"?

- Will you trust God to use all the pain of your past to give you compassion for those around you who are hurting and to use the strengths of your past to equip you to be effective in His kingdom, and will you care more about His reputation than your own?

When we see the beauty, majesty, and choice of a loving God, we let go of our arrogance and shame.

When we see the beauty, majesty, and choice of a loving God, we let go of our arrogance and shame. We feel profound relief to know we're forgiven and loved—not because of our performance, but because love is God's very nature. In response, we adore Him. We don't treat Him like a butler, a businessman, a vending machine, or Santa Claus. We worship Him in the beauty of His holiness. More than anything else, we long to please Him, to honor Him, to make Him smile. When we pray, we're not just going through a list and checking off boxes. We share our hearts so much that we might not even remember to ask Him for anything! And our motivation to obey is revolutionized. Obeying for the wrong reasons feeds our pride, and when we fail, we're devastated by shame—but it's beautiful when we obey for the right reasons.

Since Jesus walked the earth, Christians have often drifted away from an authentic relationship with Him and tried to reduce faith to a set of rules or a list of routines. Spiritual disciplines can be quantified and measured, and they can be helpful practices to shape our pursuit of God—but we have to be careful that they don't replace our heart's pursuit of God. When God becomes manageable, we're in trouble . . . we've missed Him. The writer to the Hebrews reminds us to "keep our eyes on Jesus"—not rules, not people, not rituals, not performance, not past failures or future hopes, at least not at the focal point of our sight. When anything or anyone but Jesus takes center stage, things get weird and heavy very fast. A relationship with the awesome God of the universe, the conquering King and the compassionate Servant is never boring, and He's never under our control. In a dynamic relationship of love, God is always saying and doing something fresh. The God who gave His life for us planned great things for us before time began, and He's constantly in motion. Do we notice? Do we expect less than this? When we reduce our relationship with Christ to an hour on Sunday morning or a routine we can check off each day, we miss the experience of a lifetime with the only One who will ever love us utterly and completely.

Don't let your walk with God go into a "coast mode" of empty rules and dry routines. It can be the greatest romance of your life and a working partnership to transform people's lives! If you want to be in complete control, then find another religion or philosophy. Jesus our King is far beyond our control, but we're never out of His reach.

The Bigger Picture

If we step back a bit, we see a much bigger picture of our lives and God's desire for us. The Scriptures give us the remarkable truth that we are always in the presence of Almighty God. He knows every thought in our minds, every motive that drives us, and every choice we make. This can be good news or bad news! He's watching us when we're in the boardroom and the bedroom, when we're without our family, at work, and with friends, and when we think we're alone. But we're never really alone. We're never out of God's thoughts, never out of His sight, and never off His heart.

It's easy to compartmentalize our lives into the spiritual part and the secular part, but that's not how God sees it. Everything we do can be done for the glory of God . . . or to fulfill selfish goals. In his letter to the Ephesians, Paul told employees to do their work "with sincerity of heart, just as you would obey Christ." And he told employers to treat their workers with the same respect, knowing they were accountable to Christ (Eph. 6:5-9). With God, there are no insignificant moments. Every second is an opportunity to please God or grieve Him. One of the marks of authentic love for God is our willingness to meet needs when no one is looking. In a parable about the final judgment, the King praised people who reached out to those who were hungry, thirsty, homeless, naked, sick, and imprisoned. The people he praised were surprised when the King told them, "I tell you the truth, whatever you did for one of the least of these brothers of mine, you did for me" (Matt. 25:40). Do we see every person in our lives as a representation of Christ? If we do, we'll treat them with more respect, kindness, and genuine affection.

Every event in our lives is a message from God. Riches, promotions, and blessings of all kinds shout of His goodness and generosity. Hardships and heartaches remind us of our desperate need for Him. In every situation—wonderful, boring, or tragic—God is inviting us to come to Him, seek His heart, and depend on Him a little bit more. No matter how much we know Him, there's far, far more of Him that we haven't yet seen. At every new discovery of the greatness and grace of God, our desire to know Him grows even more. In his book, *The Pursuit of God*, A. W. Tozer observes, "To have found God and still to pursue Him is the soul's paradox of love, scorned indeed by the too-easily-satisfied religionists, but justified in happy experience by the children of the burning heart."[10]

> **Every event in our lives is a message from God. Riches, promotions, and blessings of all kinds shout of His goodness and generosity. Hardships and heartaches remind us of our desperate need for Him.**

As wonderful as it is to delight in Jesus today, the Bible promises that someday, we'll see Him face to face. The sweep of biblical history will come around to where it began, with God walking with His people in a garden, but this time, it will be with far more people in the new heaven and new earth. Jesus has already *inaugurated* His kingdom on earth, but then, we will enjoy its *ultimate fulfillment*. Everything we do today to honor the King will make a difference then. In his book, *Following Jesus*, N. T. Wright, British author and professor, explains the connection between our choices today and our destiny in God's presence:

> Every act of justice, every word of truth, every creation of genuine beauty, every act of sacrificial love, will be reaffirmed on the last day, in the new world. The poem that glimpses truth in a new way, the mug of tea given with gentleness to the down-and-out at the drop-in center; the setting aside of my own longings in order to support and cherish someone who depends on me; the piece of work done honestly and thoroughly; the prayer that comes from heart and mind together; all of these and many more are building blocks for the kingdom. We may not yet see how they will fit into God's eventual structure, but the fact of the resurrection, of God's glad reaffirmation of true humanness, assures us that they will.[11]

Are you getting ready for that day? Are you experiencing God's delight now and anticipating knowing Him even more then? If you are, you're a real disciple.

Consider This

1. After reading this chapter, how would you define and describe "self-justification"? Describe the two different forms: pride and shame. How do these poison us?

2. Have you ever experienced a time of brokenness? If you have, how did God get your attention? How did you respond? What lessons did you learn?

3. Look over the list of confessions. How would it help you to use them (or something like them) to retrain your thinking and remind you of God's grace?

4. Why is it so easy to drift toward following rules and rituals instead of experiencing a rich relationship with Jesus? What's the value, then, of spiritual disciplines, like regular Bible study, prayer, worship, and service?

5. What does it mean to be "a child of the burning heart"? Are you one of those people? Do you want to be? Explain your answer.

6. How does it shape your choices today to realize there will be a glorious future in the new heaven and new earth?

chapter 6

No "Easy Button"

To live in the past and future is easy. To live in the present is like threading a needle.

Walker Percy

L et me tell the rest of the story about the time I was screaming at the windshield of my car because I was so frustrated with God's apparent inactivity. The progress of my dreams in ministry seemed to be stuck in the mud. I'd prayed, talked, and hoped something wonderful would happen so I could step out and plant a new church, but all I got from God was silence. For months, I'd waited patiently. I went over passages of Scripture, and I told God I trusted Him for the right answer at the right time. Slowly, the level of my "faith tank" drained down. On that day, my patience with God had run completely dry.

One of those verses I reviewed is Hebrews 10:35-36, which reads, "Do not throw away your confidence; it will be richly rewarded. You need to persevere so that when you have done the will of God, you will receive what he has promised." My good friend Ron Heitman and I had made this verse our theme for our junior year in college. We encouraged each other to "persevere for provision." It sounded great at the time: faith-filled, motivational, encouraging. But now, I actually had to live this verse out, and it was extremely difficult.

Several weeks after my windshield moment with God, my senior pastor accepted an offer from a church in California. It was a total surprise that he would make a move like this because he was the founding pastor of our church and had served over twenty years. Before he decided to leave, the season of infighting and division had ended, and the church appeared to be more stable. He had weathered the storm. When things looked better, I stopped thinking about leaving. I was fully prepared to support his leadership and remain as his assistant for as long as God wanted me to be there. Then, all of the sudden, he resigned.

Our church board asked me to fill in as the temporary pastor. (Actually, I was their only option because the other staff had transitioned off of the team.) I was reluctant because I didn't feel qualified. This began a season of what I call "unexpected promotion and provision." I didn't have any ambition to become the senior pastor of our church, which at the time had about 700 regular attendees. It was too large, and I was too green. Besides, my dream was to plant a church in a city that was in need—not to be a pastor of an existing congregation. In my dreams, I couldn't have imagined what happened next.

For five months, I served as temporary pastor. During this time, I looked forward to the moment when the board would identify the candidate for senior pastor so I could pass the baton and move on. But God had other plans. The board met a number of times, but after a while, they were still stuck. They couldn't agree on any of the candidates. Unexpectedly, one of them suggested that I be interviewed to fill the role. Within a few minutes, they had unanimously voted to ask me to be the candidate to present to the church. When they told me, I was dumbfounded. I couldn't believe it! I was only twenty-seven years old. I had only preached about twenty sermons in my life. I'd never led a board meeting, performed a wedding, presided over a funeral, or done any other things that senior pastors do.

As I look back on this season, I realize my plans for my ministry were much smaller than God's desire and design. When I was so frustrated and angry with God that day in the car, I can imagine God smiling and asking, "Jeff, can't you wait a couple of weeks? I'm going to answer your prayers, but not in the way you expect. If you can be patient a little longer, you're going to have a much bigger opportunity than you ever dreamed. I know you can't see it, but I've been at work for a long time preparing you and the situation. It's going to be great! Please, trust me."

I never did get to plant the church of my dreams. But God had other things in store for me.

As I write these words some twenty-one years later, I realize I never did get to plant the church of my dreams. But God had other things in store for me. Allison Park Church, where I've served as Senior Pastor, has helped to plant seventeen new churches and has a plan in motion to plant 100 churches in the next ten years. I was dreaming of planting one church, but God had so much more in mind.

Shaping Expectations

A national office supply company has run an ad in which customers can't figure out the solutions to problems at work . . . until someone shows them an "easy button," which magically connects them to products that meet their needs. I wish life were like that, not just for paper clips and copier supplies, but for marriage, parenting, careers, purpose, and everything else that really matters. Wouldn't it be great if we could push a button to fix our finances, our spouses, our kids, our health, and our hearts?

Unfortunately, sometimes we think we've found "easy buttons" in the Scriptures. Some of us read Matthew 6:33 and assume that "all these things will be added" to us effortlessly. The promises of God are wonderful and trustworthy, but they seldom happen instantly or easily. The focal point of the promise isn't the *blessings* on the back end; it's our heartfelt *pursuit* of God and His kingdom on the front end. Obedience doesn't result in an easy, pain-free life. Instead, it aligns our hearts and our lives with God and His kingdom. Being aligned with God means we care about the things He cares about, we're willing to go where He leads, and we're willing to sacrifice to accomplish His purposes. God is in motion, He has divine (and often mysterious) purposes, and our task is to keep in step with Him. It's anything but easy!

When we say yes to put God's kingdom first, we agree to follow Christ wherever He leads us. There are no guarantees of an easy path—and we sometimes can't even find the path.

His leading will eventually take us to places we don't want to go, to people who make us uncomfortable, and into circumstances that threaten us to the core. Our peace doesn't come from the absence of problems, but from holding His hand even in the darkness, even on the side of a cliff, even when we hear lions roar. God really isn't interested in our comfort, but on building our character as we learn to prioritize His leadership in our lives.

Our peace doesn't come from the absence of problems, but from holding His hand even in the darkness, even on the side of a cliff, even when we hear lions roar.

Many pastors (including yours truly) have sometimes been guilty of over-promoting the benefits and over-simplifying the process of the Christian life. Some good-hearted preachers and teachers promise an easier path than God has in mind, and a few make exorbitant promises of tangible blessings of money, cars, and houses. Certainly, the biblical principle of sowing and reaping (see Gal. 6:7–8) is a foundational concept in spiritual life, but God doesn't guarantee when or how we'll reap what we sow.

The promises of God are all true—God doesn't lie—but we often misunderstand the processes of God.

Four Phases of a Safari

When I talk about the promises and processes of God, I call it a journey. Once when I was speaking in Africa, the translator used the term *safari*, which is the Swahili term for "journey." That's what we're on: a safari with God, an adventure full of wonder and danger. If we notice the pattern in the Bible and in our own lives, we'll often see four distinct phases: the promise, problems, perseverance, and provision.

The Promise

God chose Abram to be the founder of the Hebrew nation and promised to make him "into a great nation" (Gen. 12:2). God told Abram, "Those who bless you will be blessed, and those who curse you will be cursed." Then He promised Abram that he and his descendants would bless all the nations on earth. Abram was probably thrilled at the prospect of receiving this promise, but he realized he had two big problems: First, he didn't have any children to carry his lineage, much less become a great nation. And second, he and his wife, Sarai, were well past the time to have children. (Abram was seventy-five and his wife was about sixty-five.) God had given a clear promise, but for years, Abram and Sarai remained childless.

Several years later, Abram rescued his nephew Lot, who had been carried away as a refugee in a local tribal war. Abram rallied his household servants and rode out to rescue Lot. On the way back from battle, he and God celebrated the victory, and God told him, "Do not be afraid, Abram. I am your shield, your very great reward" (Gen. 15:1).

We often sing, pray, and talk about belonging to God; but here, God says to Abram, "I belong to you! I'm your protector and provider, and my love makes you incredibly wealthy!"

Abram, though, had other things on his priority list. To God's outburst of affection, he complained, "Thanks a lot, God, but you're forgetting something. Sarai and I are childless. In case you have forgotten, you promised we'd have a child. So far, nothing. God, I've put your kingdom first, but the thing you promised hasn't been added to me. If you don't come through, a distant relative will inherit all we have. Is that what you want?" Abram was glad to have God's favor, but his heart ached for a son—the son God had promised years before.

We learn something from Abram's life. The journey of a relationship with God most often begins with this first phase: receiving a promise. God's invitation to join Him typically begins with a promise. God promised Abram a son and a nation. He promised Moses that He'd use him to free His people from the pharaoh, He gave Joseph two dreams about his future, and the prophet Samuel anointed the shepherd boy David to become the leader of Israel. All of these promises came out of the blue—at least, that's the way they seemed from the human side of things.

Problems

Immediately after each of these people received promises from God, they stepped right into a massive, messy, and seemingly impossible set of problems. Actually, this is the second phase in the safari. We receive a promise from God, but instead of finding immediate fulfillment, we step right into an enormous and unexpected problem. It feels like we've run into a brick wall. We were totally enthused about receiving the promise from God, and we were ready to see it fulfilled. We took off running, only to find ourselves flat on our backs from the impact of these unexpected obstacles.

The story in Genesis records that Abram received a promise of a son and then ran straight into a season of increasing age and infertility. Abram remained childless for years. His story isn't unique.

Years later, Joseph received an amazing dream from God that his entire family would bow down before him. But Joseph's brothers despised him and his dream. They sold him to a passing caravan. Soon, he was sold into slavery in Egypt and then thrown into prison for many years.

After God's people endured 400 years of slavery, Moses, hearing an audible voice from a burning bush, received a call from God Himself. He mustered the courage to go back to Egypt and face Pharaoh, but even his own people didn't believe God had sent him. After his first encounter with Pharaoh, things went from bad to worse. Pharaoh demanded the same quota of bricks from his slaves, but this time he didn't give them any straw. They had to find the straw themselves to fill the quota of bricks. Now, they had two backbreaking jobs instead of one! They weren't happy with Moses.

Many years later, Samuel anointed David the new king of God's people. His career started off well, but it quickly went south. David boldly killed the giant Goliath, but within days, King Saul was so jealous that he tried to pin the boy against the wall with his spear!

All of these people could have looked back at God and complained, "Hey, what's up with this? God, you gave me a promise, and I assumed you'd pave the way to make it happen."

God always has a bigger, wider, deeper picture of our future. He knows that giving the promise is only a first step on a long safari—a story that has a complex plot. Occasionally,

God fulfills a promise quickly, but far more often, He takes a circuitous route. When we encounter difficulties, we need to remember the stories of brave men and women in the Bible and in church history. They received wonderful promises from God, but most of them faced daunting obstacles, opposition, setbacks, and heartaches.

God always has a bigger, wider, deeper picture of our future. He knows that giving the promise is only a first step on a long safari—a story that has a complex plot.

We like the idea of a resurrection, but there's something that must happen first: death. In some instances, the problems we face after God gives us a promise aren't bumps in the road. The bridge crumbles into the river! At that moment, we feel confused and deeply disappointed. Some people who have walked closely with God describe such points in their lives as "the death of a dream." They prayed, they asked God for wisdom, they received a promise, and they believed He was leading them to do wonderful things for the kingdom. They worked hard and prayed hard, but at a pivotal point, the bottom dropped out. Everything they tried failed, and their prayers seemed to bounce off heaven. Their hopes, their desires, their dreams died. They felt abandoned . . . crushed. If they refused to give up on God, though, He led them to something new. It wasn't the same dream as before. It was different: deeper, purified, and better. They had suffered through a painful and confusing death, but God resurrected their hopes and gave them something more wonderful than they ever dreamed.

No one likes to go through a death, but if we don't, we'll never enjoy a resurrection. My out-of-control moment in the car was when I faced the death of my dream. I had wanted God to lead me on a career path that made sense to me. I'd been preparing, hoping, and waiting. There were many options that seemed perfectly valid to me, but none of them panned out. I thought I had it all mapped out. My plans seemed perfect to me, but they weren't God's best. My dream had to die so He could prepare me for something far better.

Perseverance

If we don't understand the processes of God, we may be tempted to give up before we see the fulfillment of the promise. If we read between the lines in the lives of Abram, Moses, Joseph, and David, we can easily understand that they sometimes felt like giving up on God. The delays they faced weren't a few hours or days; they were sometimes decades. The difficulties they faced weren't minor; they were life threatening. They may have wanted to walk away dozens of times, but they didn't. They didn't stop clinging to God. They held on to the hope that someday, somehow, He would fulfill His promises. Remember, the writer to the Hebrews tells us, "So do not throw away your confidence; it will be richly rewarded. You need to persevere so that when you have done the will of God, you will receive what he has promised" (Heb. 10:35–36).

Perseverance isn't just about time—it's about enduring difficulties with tenacious faith. It's clinging to God's promise in spite of the lack of visible evidence. We obey, pray, and stand strong in steadfast hope even though everything we see is the opposite of what we expected. We rivet our minds on the truths of God's Word, and we fasten our hearts on His character of love, forgiveness, power, wisdom, and understanding. We may not see the answer yet, but we're sure God will give it in His way and in His time.

> **We obey, pray, and stand strong in steadfast hope even though everything we see is the opposite of what we expected.**

Perseverance, though, isn't just about gritting our teeth. In times of waiting and suffering, God wants to do a deep work in our hearts to purify our motives, deepen our dependence on Him, and refocus our hope. During these difficult times, we realize more than ever that Jesus paid an enormous price to do the Father's will—not only on the cross, but in honoring the Father all day, every day when He experienced opposition and misunderstanding. What does perseverance look like for us? Paul told the Corinthians, "We always carry around in our body the death of Jesus, so that the life of Jesus may also be revealed in our body" (2 Cor. 4:10). Eventually, God uses the phase of waiting and trusting to refocus our hope in Him and the things that really matter. In the process, God gives us new lenses so we see more clearly. Paul concluded, "Therefore we do not lose heart. Though outwardly we are wasting away, yet inwardly we are being renewed day by day. For our light and momentary troubles are achieving for us an eternal glory that far outweighs them all. So we fix our eyes not on what is seen, but on what is unseen. For what is seen is temporary, but what is unseen is eternal" (2 Cor. 4:16-18). As we wait, we need new eyes to see the bigger, eternal picture.

But why? Why does God choose this method of relating to His people? Can't He come up with a better way? We sure can! Sometimes, I pray, "God, I don't get it. You're the God of the universe. You can do anything. You've given me a promise, so I know you want to accomplish it. Why the delay and difficulty before I get to the destination?"

Over the years, I believe God has given me two answers to my questions. First, in times of waiting and struggle, God wants to deepen our *faith* in Him. Faith is the conviction of what is true in the absence of visible evidence, so delays and difficulties are the fertile soil where faith can grow. The longer the delay and the greater the difficulties, the more our faith can flourish. When weightlifters want to grow stronger, they use heavier weights and more repetitions. As they encounter more resistance over a longer period, their muscles get stronger. It's the same with muscles of faith. We press against the problems in our life as we stand in persevering faith. As we stand strong, our "faith muscles" develop, and we become stronger than ever.

Faith is the conviction of what is true in the absence of visible evidence, so delays and difficulties are the fertile soil where faith can grow. The longer the delay and the greater the difficulties, the more our faith can flourish.

The second reason God causes us to wait for the promise to be fulfilled is to teach us how to *fight*. We don't live in a static world; we live in a war zone. The forces of darkness are all around us. They use temptation, accusation, and deception to get us off track. To counter their lies and schemes, we have to put on our spiritual armor and fight. We're not empty handed, and we aren't alone. Paul reminded the Corinthians, "For though we live in the world, we do not wage war as the world does. The weapons we fight with are not the weapons of the world. On the contrary, they have divine power to demolish strongholds. We demolish arguments and every pretension that sets itself up against the knowledge of God, and we take captive every thought to make it obedient to Christ" (2 Cor. 10:3–5). As we continue to pray and obey, we're fighting side by side with God and other believers against the forces of the enemy. In *The Fight*, psychiatrist and Vineyard speaker John White shares his views:

> You have established a new relationship with the powers of darkness. Whatever you were before you were a Christian . . . you are now a sworn foe of the legions of hell. Have no delusions about their reality or their hostility. But do not fear them. The God inside you terrifies them. They cannot touch you, let alone hurt you. But they can still seduce, and they will try. They will also oppose you as you obey Christ. . . . But if you are serious about Christ being your Lord and God, you can expect opposition.[12]

When Abram was ninety-nine years old, God changed his name to Abraham. He had waited for twenty-four years, and he was still waiting . . . but God gave him a confession of faith. He was no longer to be called Abram (which means "daddy"); he would now be Abraham (which is "big daddy," the father of many nations). To legally change his name, Abraham had to go to the local courts. They may have looked at him and thought he'd lost his mind. They might have said, "Look, Abe, you've been talking about this for twenty-four years. Come on. Be realistic. You don't need to change your name to coincide with the promise. Give it up, old man." But Abraham didn't give up. Every time he said his new name, he confessed his renewed faith in God's promise.

This is how we fight. We use the primary weapon God has given us, which is His Word, and we use it as a weapon to defeat the forces of darkness. His promise becomes the "sword of the Spirit" in our mouths. We confess and declare what God has promised, and our declarations of faith shake the heavens. Every moment we persevere in the promise of God, we do spiritual battle to defeat the resistance of demonic forces and release the will and purpose of God on the earth.

The Promise Fulfilled

Finally, after disappointments, delays, and some huge mistakes, Abraham and Sarah had a baby boy. They named him Isaac, which means "laughter." When God fulfills His promise in our lives, we throw our heads back and laugh out loud. We tell everyone who will listen (and maybe a few who'd rather not), "Isn't this fantastic! Let me tell you what God did." Isn't this amazing? A hundred-year-old man and a ninety-year-old woman had a miracle baby! Even God had a good chuckle at that one. It was a beautiful, amazing God-moment.

Moses persevered through ten plagues, Pharaoh's taunts, and forty years of complaints, dust, and sweat to take God's people to the brink of the Promised Land.

Joseph had dreamed that his parents and brothers would someday bow down to him, but he had no idea it would occur when he was the prime minister of the most powerful nation on earth. God took him from the darkest dungeon and put him at the pinnacle of power. There, he predicted a great famine and administrated the rationing of grain to keep people alive through seven long years of drought. Some of the people who survived were his father, his brothers, and their families. They owed him their lives.

David had several opportunities to kill Saul and claim the throne, but he refused. He and his men ran like crazy to escape, and finally, David became the new king on the throne. God used the young shepherd to unite the people and build a strong kingdom. This is the moment we dream about and pray for—it's the provision of the promise. This is our favorite part of the story. God fulfills His promise. God provides for our needs. No matter how long it takes, God will do what He has promised. You can count on it. We look forward to seeing our "Isaacs" born into the world. Then we can throw our heads back and just belly laugh at the goodness of God. But there's a risk in the last phase of the safari.

> **If we're not careful, though, we can get so focused on the provision that we elevate the value of the *provision* higher than we value the *Provider*.**

Be Careful

It's a wonderful, amazing, hilarious thing when God finally meets our deepest desires and fulfills His promises. If we're not careful, though, we can get so focused on the provision that we elevate the value of the *provision* higher than we value the *Provider*. We begin to think, *As soon as this provision is mine, my life will be complete. As soon as the healing comes, or I meet Mr. or Ms. Right, or I get the job I want, or we get the child we're praying for, then I'll be totally fulfilled.* If we aren't careful, we can put the provision in our hearts in place of God, making the answer to our prayers into an idol. That's what happened to Abraham.

About twelve years after Isaac was born, the old dad became too attached to his son. It happens. In fact, we don't have to be a hundred years old and a patriarch of the faith to put our kids in the wrong place in our hearts. Plenty of parents do it. God loved Abraham too much to let him stay off base, so He gave the old man the most bizarre, gut-wrenching command uttered in the Bible: Take the boy to a mountain and sacrifice him there. God had no intention of Abraham killing his son. It was a test—a big and necessary test of Abraham's primary affection.

This was an excruciating moment in Abraham's life. God asked him to place the provision of the promise—his son Isaac—on the altar to demonstrate that he valued the Provider more than the provision. And he passed the test. He was willing to obey God, no matter the cost. When he picked up the knife, an angel of the Lord stopped him. He told the relieved dad, "Now I know that you fear God, because you have not withheld from me your son, your only son" (Gen. 22:12). In Isaac's place on the altar, God provided a ram in the thicket for the sacrifice.

Sooner or later, it's the same for each of us. God tests us to see if we care more about the provision or the Provider. These moments are turning points in our lives. Will we be ready to face them with the courage and trust Abraham displayed?

What's Next?

When I teach about the phases of a safari, people often assume that phase four is the end of the journey. We receive the promise, we face the problem, we choose to persevere, and finally, we receive the provision. I always ask the audience, "What's next? After receiving what God has promised, then what? Is life perfect? Are there no more problems? Is everything easy? Are we done?"

When we reach the end of the process, we loop back to the beginning. We get to start the safari with God again as He gives us a new promise. Often, the promise is even bigger, so we step into a bigger problem. God knows He can trust us with more because our faith has grown and is ready. This requires a season of perseverance. Then finally, once again, we experience God's wonderful provision. And when that safari is complete, we get to go back to the beginning again. This safari process never stops until we arrive at the ultimate provision of eternal life. As long as we live in this earthly body,

> **Often, the promise is even bigger, so we step into a bigger problem. God knows He can trust us with more because our faith has grown and is ready.**

we'll be on a safari in one phase or another. Actually, it's possible to be on several safaris at the same time. We may be at the promise phase in one area of life, such as our career, marriage, kids, or ministry, and in the perseverance phase in another.

Continually being on a safari sounds exhausting, doesn't it? Long seasons of perseverance are especially grueling. In these times, it's tempting to look for a way out, but we choose to keep walking, keep trusting, and keep hoping. Where do we find strength to keep going?

When we're in the middle of the safari, we don't focus our minds and hearts on the promise, the process, or the provision, but on God, our provider. Wherever we are on the journey, God is more than enough. Somewhere in the middle of all this, we'll realize that we don't care nearly as much about the promise as we thought. We'll understand that God is our shield and our great reward. The promise and the provision are wonderful, but it's far more wonderful to experience the love, presence, power, and purpose of God Himself. Abraham didn't just get a son. He got a relationship with God that we're still talking about four thousand years later. Moses didn't just get a mission; he met God, talked with Him, and watched Him work. Joseph wasn't just a mechanical instrument to save some lives during a time of famine. He connected with God so closely that God gave him his greatest dream—a relationship with the God of glory. And David was called "a man after God's own heart." His psalms describe a vibrant, authentic connection with God, sometimes in praise, sometimes in sorrow, always in awe.

Wherever you are in your journey, your focus should not be on the next phase in the journey. It should be an upward gaze toward your Father and Provider. Reach up to Him. Place your hand in His. Let Him lead you through this process. He will never leave you and never forsake you. His grace is more than enough. As you trust Him in the process, you step into a life that truly has a sense of greatness about it.

When we read through the Bible, we can't find a single person who was called by God to something easy. Every hero of faith in Hebrews 11 faced incalculable obstacles. They are heroes precisely because they conquered great problems and trusted God in the darkness. That's what heroes do.

No one tells stories about pushing the easy button in their lives and taking the easy way out. But our imaginations hang on the stories of common people trusting God to do uncommon things. Those are the stories that thrill our hearts.

When people I love and respect tell me stories about their lives, they don't talk about the pleasant days they spent at theme parks. They talk about the biggest difficulties they've faced, the heartaches they've endured, and the occasions God has seen them through in the nick of time. You and I are creating stories today, legacies for our children and grandchildren. What kind of stories will they hear? Will we tell them about the latest car we bought, the vacation we took, or the television shows we watched? Probably not. We don't want to bore them to death! I want to tell my kids about the long safaris, the breakthrough miracles, and the times when God's presence was so real I could almost reach out and touch Him. To have real faith, we have to journey down challenging paths. There are no other roads that lead to God.

Near the end of His most famous message, Jesus explained that not everyone wants to go on the adventure of a spiritual safari. He told the crowd, "Enter through the narrow gate. For wide is the gate and broad is the road that leads to destruction, and many enter through it. But small is the gate and narrow the road that leads to life, and only a few find it" (Matt. 7:13–14). Most people want to use the easy button in their lives, but it puts them on the wrong road. It's wide at first, but it leads to emptiness, strained relationships, and destruction. It's popular. We see it depicted on television and in ads all day, every day. The other way, which is God's path, looks cramped and difficult at first, but it leads to more joy, strength, and purpose than we ever dreamed possible. And the people we meet on this road support us as we take courageous steps. Jesus said that "few find" the narrow road. It may not be an easy one, but it's the right one. It may not be popular, but I'm on it. Will you join me? (You probably already have, or you wouldn't have read this far.)

Consider This

1. What are some of your favorite ads? What is the product or service? What is the hidden promise that the product or service will do for people?

2. When we're watching or listening to advertisements, what questions can we ask so we're more astute to observe the promise of "the ideal life"?

3. What are some promises God gives people who follow Him? What is a promise He has given you? How have you responded to it?

4. How would you describe "the death of a dream"? How does God use problems in our lives after He's given us a promise?

5. God uses a time of perseverance to develop our *faith* and equip us to *fight*. Do you know someone who has persevered by trusting God for a long time? What do you admire about that person?

6. What are some stories your family tells? Which ones amaze you or inspire you?

7. What kind of stories are you telling your kids (or which kind do you want to tell them)?

chapter 7

A Word from God

**By reading the scriptures I am so renewed that
all nature seems renewed around me and with
me. The sky seems to be a pure, a cooler blue, the
trees a deeper green. The whole world is charged
with the glory of God and I feel fire and music
under my feet.**

Thomas Merton

To move forward with God, we need a word from Him.
We don't just launch out on our own to make a spiritual
safari. We need directions from our Guide. He gives us a
message, and everything comes from His Word: faith, courage, hope, love, and tenacity. If we pay attention, God brings
passages of Scripture to mind. When I was feeling so anxious
in college, God reminded me of a passage I'd never memo-
rized and couldn't remember ever hearing taught before. I'm
sure I'd read it many times, but until that crucial, vulnerable
moment, it hadn't meant much to me. Suddenly, it meant
everything. I was wrestling with intense feelings of guilt
and shame (and losing), but God gave me His Word from
Romans: "Anyone who trusts in him will never be put to
shame." This message from God was a lifeline to a drowning

young man. I don't know what would have happened if God hadn't connected truth and hope to my heart at that pivotal moment in my life.

Getting a Word

Some Christians treat the Bible as if it contains some kind of plague bacilli. They keep it on the shelf far away from their daily lives. Others believe it's a magic potion. They flip it open and hope their finger will land on a verse that meets their need at a particular moment. The Bible, though, is a living letter from God to us. The Holy Spirit uses it to transform lives. It has the power to confront our secrets and comfort our pain. It calls to our hearts and elicits the highest praise and genuine contrition. The writer to the Hebrews described the Scriptures with graphic language: "For the word of God is living and active. Sharper than any double-edged sword, it penetrates even to dividing soul and spirit, joints and marrow; it judges the thoughts and attitudes of the heart. Nothing in all creation is hidden from God's sight. Everything is uncovered and laid bare before the eyes of him to whom we must give account" (Heb. 4:12–13). Are we letting God wield His sword in our lives like a surgeon's scalpel? That's what He wants to do—but not to hurt us. Like a surgeon, God cuts us so He can heal us.

Faith is trust in the absence of things *seen* (Heb. 11:1), but genuine faith can't exist in the absence of things *heard*. Paul told the Romans, "Faith comes from hearing the message, and the message is heard through the word of Christ" (Rom. 10:17). Paul wrote his protégé Timothy to encourage him. Timothy's mother and grandmother had taught him God's Word. Paul reminded him of the multiple ways God uses His Word in the lives of His children: "All Scripture is God-breathed and is useful for teaching, rebuking, correcting and training in righteousness, so that the man of God may be thoroughly equipped for every good work" (2 Tim. 3:16–17). Do we want to get ahead in every aspect of life? Paul says the Bible is profitable to teach us God's truth, show us how we fall short, get us back on track with kingdom purposes, and help us develop habits that make us useful in God's strong and loving hands. When we come to the Scriptures, that's what God wants to do in our lives. When we open the pages of the Bible, what do we expect from Him and His Word?

I heard a story years ago about four men who loved to play golf. They planned and saved for a year to travel to a course they all dreamed of playing. When they arrived and went out to the first tee, a dense fog shrouded the landscape. They could only see a few feet in front of them. They thought about going back to the clubhouse and calling it a day, but they wanted to find some way to play a round of golf. One of them had an idea. He walked down the fairway some distance and yelled back to the guys on the tee. He said, "Hit the ball toward the sound of my voice!" The men played the front nine this way, and to their astonishment, they actually played very well. After the first nine, the sun began to burn off the fog, the clouds lifted, and the men stood in bright sunlight. As they played the back nine, they reverted back to their old habits of hooking and slicing the ball. Their scores soared when they played golf by sound because they were more focused, more deliberate, and more careful to hit the ball toward their friend who yelled from down the fairway or from the green. They played better when they played by sound instead of by sight. I don't know if this story is true, but it illustrates the impact of the written or spoken word to get our attention, focus our minds, and draw the best out of us. We reach toward an invisible God, but He's not silent. He calls to us from the Scriptures, and the Holy Spirit opens the eyes of our hearts so we grasp the significance of each truth and apply it to our lives. Faith is following the voice of God.

Faith is following the voice of God.

The word God gave me in my season of anxiety isn't an isolated instance. When I considered planting churches, God led me to the promise in Matthew 6:33. I realized that if I put God and His kingdom first in my life, God would unleash the power of heaven to accomplish His purposes through me. At another time, I was completely burned out by the worries of tangled staff relationships, financial pressures, and family challenges. I'd been working hard to keep all of the plates spinning, but I was exhausted. One morning, I was praying about all these things, and God led me to the opening verses of Paul's second letter to the Corinthians. There I read, "We do not want you to be uninformed, brothers, about the hardships we suffered in the province of Asia. We were under great pressure, far beyond our ability to endure, so that we despaired even of life. Indeed, in our hearts we felt the sentence of death. But this happened that we might not rely on ourselves but on God, who raises the dead" (2 Cor. 1:8–9). I realized this was Paul writing about his experience of struggling under intense pressures. His strain was so tough that he thought he might die! Paul's encouragement—to the Corinthians and to me that morning—was that the struggles we face have a God-designed purpose: to teach us to rely on God instead of ourselves. *Okay*, I thought, *if that's how God wants to use all these problems, I'm up for it.* I could rely on the "God who raises the dead" to give me peace, confidence, and direction to face my worries.

I grew up in the most loving, fun, supportive home anyone can imagine, but one day when I was five, my world came crashing down. My little sister was born! What? Yes, I had been the little man of the house, the center of attention, and now, I had to share my parents' affection. I resented her and everything about her! Of course, I didn't understand that at the time, but it was true. A few years later (when she was five and I was ten), she developed juvenile diabetes, and my mom and dad gave her the necessary care for her condition. In my own selfish view of life, however, I resented her even more. Horrible, I know. Bitterness was firmly rooted in my young heart, and it started to raise its ugly head. When I was in middle school, the boiling cauldron of bitterness spilled out almost every day. I was dealing with raging hormones, conflicting emotions about my identity, and mounting frustrations of all kinds. My anger needed an outlet, so I tormented my sister. I tried to bury my emotions, but unfortunately, the anger didn't stay buried for long. It came out in fits of temper that grew so strong that I sometimes astonished myself. Today, I look back at those teenage years, and I have only one explanation for the way I felt and acted. It wasn't that my sister had done anything to me. It wasn't that my parents had neglected or abused me. I had a fantastic life with an amazing family. The only reason for my pervasive resentment and temper was pure selfishness. I didn't want to be this way, but bitterness had grabbed my soul. I was the perfect pastor's kid in public, but when others weren't looking, I was emotionally explosive, punching holes in walls, breaking appliances, and making my family— especially my sister—miserable. Later, I found out my mother and father often asked each other, "What are we going to do with Jeff?" They had no idea how to corral my temper. I didn't either.

I came to Christ when I was fifteen, but the bitterness didn't vanish. I began to lead Bible Studies for other students in my home, and yet the seething anger was still there. God called me into ministry, and I went to Bible College, and yet still the internalized hurt and anger was like a weight on my soul. A few years later, Melodie and I began dating. After being together for about three months, our relationship had some problems. I didn't know how to handle disagreements, and I overreacted to a relatively minor misunderstanding. At one point, she looked at me and asked, "What's up with you? This isn't a big deal, but you're making it into one." After a few seconds, she said, "Jeff, I don't think you're mad at me at all. I think you're still angry at your sister, but you're taking it out on me."

Instantly, I knew she had spoken the unvarnished truth. Then a realization hit me hard: If I didn't figure out how to resolve the pent up anger I'd kept inside so long, I'd never be able to have a successful relationship. Not only would I lose this woman I loved, but I would never be able to maintain a healthy relationship with anyone. The journey of learning to forgive was both hard and wonderful. The Lord led me to passages that encouraged me to deal with anger quickly

(Eph. 4:26–27), and I discovered that my ability to forgive others was based on my experience of God's forgiveness of my own sins (Eph. 4:31–32). Forgiveness is both a choice and a process. It was one of the most important words—actually, a whole constellation of words about bitterness, forgiveness, trust, and reconciliation—God has ever given me.

> **Forgiveness is both a choice and a process.**

After Melodie and I got married, all our problems vanished. No, that's a lie. Two flawed humans always have plenty of problems, and we had our share. One day, we argued about something, and I refused to even try to see her side of things. In the debate, I raised my voice. My anger was building to a point that could have gotten ugly, so I left the room, got in the car, and went for a long drive. I was fuming. After many hours in the car, it was late at night. I pulled into our driveway, walked inside, and went to bed without saying a word to her. The next morning, I got up, dressed, and went to the office—again without speaking to Melodie. As was my custom, I opened my Bible for my morning devotions. As I knelt to pray, my eyes fell on a passage in Peter's first letter: "Husbands, in the same way be considerate as you live with your wives, and treat them with respect as the weaker partner and as heirs with you of the gracious gift of life, so that nothing will hinder your prayers" (1 Pet. 3:7). I clearly sensed the Holy Spirit saying to me, "Don't even bother to pray right now. If you want me to answer any prayers, you need to get up right now, go home, and apologize to Melodie. You and I aren't doing business until you make this right."

I drove home, found Melodie, and said, "I was wrong. My attitude and my words were harsh. Will you please forgive me?" She graciously forgave me. When I got back to the office, I knelt again to pray. Because I had obeyed the voice of the Lord, His presence was there with me. It was an important moment for two relationships: with God and with Melodie.

Jesus is described in Hebrews as "the author and perfecter of our faith" (Heb. 12:2). God begins His work in our lives by giving us a word. Whatever He authors, He will be faithful to complete. I'm afraid that I—and many others—run around trying to get God to be responsible for things we want but He hasn't authored. If we are the authors, there are no promises from God that He'll jump through our hoops. However, if He initiates, we can be confident that "he who began a good work in you will carry it on to completion until the day of Christ Jesus" (Phil. 1:6). Before God asks us to do a work, He always gives us a word. If we don't have one, or we aren't clear about what it is, we need to ask Him for clarity. If we go off half-cocked in our own strength to accomplish something we think is a good thing to do, we'll meet frustration and failure. It's hard enough if we're in line with God! Why in the world would we think we could do kingdom work without a word from the King?

Jesus often used agrarian metaphors to make His point. As He walked with His disciples through a vineyard, He explained that the essence of spiritual life is being intimately connected with Him. He compared us to branches on a grape vine:

> "Remain in me, and I will remain in you. No branch can bear fruit by itself; it must remain in the vine.

Neither can you bear fruit unless you remain in me. I am the vine; you are the branches. If a man remains in me and I in him, he will bear much fruit; apart from me you can do nothing. If anyone does not remain in me, he is like a branch that is thrown away and withers; such branches are picked up, thrown into the fire and burned. If you remain in me and my words remain in you, ask whatever you wish, and it will be given you. This is to my Father's glory, that you bear much fruit, showing yourselves to be my disciples" (John 15:4-8).

When we're connected in a vital, intimate, real relationship with God, our spiritual ears become attuned to His voice, and we learn to listen for His word. When we read the Bible, we're no longer surprised when the Spirit whispers or shouts to us and a passage appears that seems to have been written for us to apply at that moment. It's a beautiful thing.

Our Diet

How can we hear from God? And how can we know if an impression means that God is speaking to us? These are important questions believers have asked for centuries. My advice is to have a constant diet of feasting on God's Word. As we read, study, listen, and pray through passages of Scripture, God's truth becomes imbedded in our

As we read, study, listen, and pray through passages of Scripture, God's truth becomes imbedded in our hearts and minds.

hearts and minds. Then, when we need a particular verse, the Spirit reminds us. We may not be able to quote it from memory, but we can find it. Then, as we meditate on it, wrestle with it, and apply it to our current situation, the exact wording becomes precious to us. Some people tell me they "can't memorize Scripture." I don't want to be unkind, but that's just not true! We all memorize dozens, even hundreds, of things that are important to us: lyrics to songs, baseball statistics, commercial jingles, etc. When the Word of God becomes as important, memorizing passages becomes second nature.

As we become more familiar with the Bible, we see patterns of history and teaching. We don't feel as lost in the Old Testament, we recognize miracles and parables in the Gospels, and we realize the churches Paul addressed in his letters had many of the same problems we have today. Some people play "Scripture roulette" and flip through the pages until they land on a verse. Yes, in His mercy, God sometimes uses even this practice to impart truth to us, but as we mature, we find more effective ways of internalizing God's Word.

Most of the instances when God has sent me a word occurred when I was already digging into the Scriptures, soaking in the truths, and inviting God to speak to me. When we have a steady diet of truth and grace, God has many opportunities to get our attention.

People often ask me, "Okay, I hear what you're saying about having a steady diet of God's Word, but where do I start?"

Great question! If someone is investigating Christianity or is new to the faith, I often suggest he or she begin by reading one of the Gospels. The gospel of John explains who

Jesus is and why He came. In fact, John clearly states his purpose for his account of Jesus' life: "Jesus did many other miraculous signs in the presence of his disciples, which are not recorded in this book. But these are written that you may believe that Jesus is the Christ, the Son of God, and that by believing you may have life in his name" (John 20:30–31). Most people love to read stories, so I suggest they read the Gospels, then Acts, and then maybe Genesis. Some of the most gripping and wonderful stories in the Bible are in the very first book.

Some time ago, I met with a new believer who asked where he should start reading in the Bible. I recommended the Gospels. He looked a bit lost, so I said, "You know: Matthew, Mark, Luke, and John."

He smiled and asked, "Okay, who are those guys? And where do I find them?"

We had a good laugh together. I opened the Bible and showed him Matthew's gospel, but I said, "Why don't you start with the shortest one?" I turned a few pages to Mark and said, "Start here. You'll love the action."

He asked, "How much do I read each day?"

"As much as you want," I explained. "Read until something stands out to you. Then stop, think about it, and then obey something God said to you through His Word. For example, if it says, 'Love your enemies,' plan to be especially kind to someone who has been unkind to you. If you have a hard time doing that, you're in good company. It takes a heart melted by grace and the power of the Spirit to obey God and follow Him into uncharted territory in relationships. If you just read it and don't obey it, your life won't change, and your faith won't grow stronger."

He sat back and took a deep breath. "That's a lot more than reading a few paragraphs!"

"Yeah, it sure is," I agreed. "Reading is important, but it's just the first step. We need to read until we find a verse or two that makes our hearts sing. Then we take it in our hands like a wet rag, squeeze it and wring every drop out of it. And when we think we've got it—or it's got us—we make the decision to obey what God says to us through it. That's what it means to 'let the word of Christ dwell in you richly.' Are you up for that?"

"Yeah," he smiled. "But I'm going to need some help along the way."

I assured him, "Hey, why do you think I'm here? I'll be glad to help."

I often recommend the *One-Year Bible*. I use it myself every day. It gives us bite-sized chunks to read every day so we complete the whole Bible in a year. As we become more comfortable with the primary themes of the Bible—some people identify them as creation, sin, redemption, and restoration— we may want to dig deep into a particular book or letter for an extended period of time. We may study Ephesians for several months, reading, praying, and talking with friends about what we've learned. By the time we're finished, the concepts of each chapter are burned into our hearts, readily accessible for the Spirit to use anytime, anywhere.

I'll admit that when a person unfamiliar with the Bible picks it up for the first few times, it's intimidating. Some people make these attempts with a thirty-pound, gilt-edged version they found on their parents' coffee table. Usually, these are written in early seventeenth century English, which is hard to understand. Invest a few bucks in a modern translation. You don't have to buy one that has a leather cover. In fact, there are many resources available online for free. For instance, you can use a terrific site, Youversion.com, on your computer, phone, iPad, or Kindle. OneyearBibleonline.com provides free Bible readings online every day. Just find a method that works for you and a version that's easy to read, and go for it.[13]

Pick Up a Pen

One of the most helpful practices in my life is journaling. Some people write so much each day it's like a chapter of a book. I don't do that. Wherever I am in my daily devotions, I find a particular verse or short passage that's meaningful to me, and I write it at the top of a page. (I have a small, 5.5 by 8.5 notebook, but almost anything will do.) As I think and pray, I jot down some reflections. The act of writing has a powerful influence on our thinking process. It causes us to be more focused. It's so easy to get distracted. If I'm not careful, my mind can drift to the worries of the day, a football score, or the carpet that needs to be cleaned. Anything can distract me! Writing helps me concentrate and go another layer deeper in my reflections on the passage.

Anything can distract me! Writing helps me concentrate and go another layer deeper in my reflections on the passage.

We can't dig deep in a single day on a large portion of Scripture. As you read broadly, ask God to give you a single verse or brief passage to be your focal point for the day. Then, wring it out like a wet rag. Think about the meaning of each word, each phrase, and each sentence. Put yourself in the text. Feel the emotions of the father whose son was possessed by a demon, but the disciples couldn't cast it out. Sense the courage of Paul as he stood in front of several trials and boldly told his accusers and judges about Jesus. Stand at the foot of the cross with the women and John as they watched the life ebb out of Jesus and heard a Roman soldier say, "Surely, this was the Son of God." When God seems to demand more than you can give, realize that He never meant for us to measure up to His standards on our own. The law was given to show us our need for grace and to deepen our trust in the power of the Holy Spirit. Don't hurry through your meditation. It's not a race, and you're not trying to cover everything in a day. Come at the Bible from both ends: broad and narrow. Read broadly to get the sweep of the whole narrative, but dig deeply into a single verse. Let it pierce your heart like an arrow and warm your spirit like the voice of your dearest friend. It's amazing how much God can impart to us through a single verse of Scripture—if we'll take the time to meditate and journal on it.

Many Christian leaders throughout the centuries have recommended different methods of journaling to enhance our devotional lives. Some are extensive, but many are quite simple. Try several to see what works for you, but try something. In his book, *Divine Mentor*, Pastor Wayne Cordiero explains a simple but effective journaling method he calls SOAP. The letters stand for Scripture, Observation, Application, and Prayer.[14] Try it. See if it works for you. Write a few sentences under each heading. Write out the Scripture verse, and make an Observation about what it meant to the original readers. Consider how it Applies to your life today.

Then turn that application into a Prayer that you write and declare to God.

In the first psalm, the writer says that if we want to experience God's blessings, we'll delight in His truth, and we'll "meditate day and night" (Ps. 1:2). The word *meditate* was familiar to shepherds of that day. It meant to "chew the cud." An animal spent a long time carefully chewing grass and then chewed it again and again until it got all the nutrients out of it. Meditating is countercultural because it can't be hurried. Most of us live at a rapid pace, but spiritual nourishment comes with patience, focus, and persistence as we chew on the truth in God's Word. We go over it and over it, and we whisper it out loud, praying and asking God to speak to us. Finally, it works its way into our spirits. When this happens, our spiritual roots grow deep, and we find ourselves "like a tree planted by streams of water, which yields its fruit in season and whose leaf does not wither" (Ps. 1:3). Isn't that what you want?

Let me give you an example. One of the most common commands and invitations of Jesus is simply, "Follow me." You can reap tremendous rewards from thinking about these two profound words. "Follow." What does it mean to follow someone? What if you are supremely confident the person knows the right direction? What if it appears the person is leading you into a blind alley . . . or over a cliff? Does following mean you can't ask questions? Does it mean you follow even when your questions don't get answers? Where did Jesus lead people? Where is He leading you? "Me." Who is this Jesus who invites you to follow Him? In what ways has He proven He is supremely trustworthy? What are the risks? Do you really trust Him enough to "leave everything" and follow Him? What does that mean anyway? Consider both of these words together: What's the next step for you as you follow Jesus?

The Bible gives us a lot of information about God, but all the truth, doctrine, and principles aren't an end in themselves. They point us to a relationship with God so that we truly know Him. The prophet Jeremiah recognized the fact that it's easy for us to pursue visible things instead of treasuring God. He wrote these words:

> This is what the LORD says: "Let not the wise man boast of his wisdom or the strong man boast of his strength or the rich man boast of his riches, but let him who boasts boast about this: that he understands and knows me, that I am the LORD, who exercises kindness, justice and righteousness on earth, for in these I delight," declares the LORD (Jer. 9:23–24).

What do I talk about? Where do I put my trust? What do I defend, and what do I boast about? God spoke through Jeremiah to say that the things that fill the minds and hearts of most people are only ashes and dust. Knowing God is far more valuable than human wisdom, strength, and wealth. Every passage of Scripture ultimately points to this supreme truth.

When we take time to think deeply about a passage, ask questions, and look from different angles, God draws us closer to His heart.

When we take time to think deeply about a passage, ask questions, and look from different angles, God draws us closer to His heart. When we know Him better, we love Him and obey Him more. That's the way spiritual life works.

Tune In

The Holy Spirit is the author of the Word of God. He loves the Word, and He loves opening our hearts to grasp its truths. Jesus told His disciples that one of the Holy Spirit's jobs is to "guide [us] into all truth" (John 16:13) and to remind us of everything that He has said (John 14:26). He is the ultimate interpreter of the Scriptures to us, and He helps us apply what we read. We have to "tune in" to hear His voice. How can we know we're in tune with the Spirit? One of the ways we can listen to the Spirit's voice is by learning to discern the *tone, temperature, and truth* of the message we hear. First, we look for tone. The Holy Spirit's tone is always supportive, positive, and loving. He may correct, but only to build and rebuild—never to crush. Experts say that 93 percent of communication is something other than the actual words. The tone of a person's voice is crucial. Two people can say, "I love you." The tone of one communicates tenderness, warmth, and sincerity, but the other is just mouthing words. Tone matters! The Holy Spirit is never harsh, condemning, or punitive. In His communication to us, the Spirit lives out His encouragement to all of us: "Do not let any unwholesome talk come out of your mouths, but only what is helpful for building others up according to their needs, that it may benefit those who listen" (Eph. 4:29).

The second signal we look for is temperature. Often, people speak of a prompting from the Holy Spirit as if they felt an inner warmth or a sense of reassurance and peace. On the contrary, when we hear the enemy's voice in our heads, we feel chilled to the bone with fear and dread. Your spirit can tell who is speaking by the inner sense of awareness God has created in you. When the Holy Spirit speaks, people sense a nudge or a prompting. Someone who loves us is near, and it feels right. We don't have to force ourselves to respond to Him; we want to respond! Words can't really describe the sensation of knowing that the God of the universe has touched our hearts, but it's very real at that moment.

This kind of communication is different from what we experience in our everyday lives. We're used to responding in relationships through tangible, visible, and audible means. We see someone with our physical eyes. We hear him or her speaking with our physical ears. We can judge who it is by these natural senses. But God speaks to us primarily "Spirit to spirit." Jesus told the woman at the well, "God is Spirit, and His worshipers must worship in spirit and in truth" (John 4:24). God is Spirit and so are we. We aren't "physical people with a spiritual dimension." We are "spiritual people with a temporary physical body." One day, our present body will die, but our spirit will continue to live. Since God is Spirit and we are spirit, it makes sense that He would speak to us Spirit to spirit. We were made for spiritual connections. It's not rare, and it's not weird. That's how we're wired. God created and crafted us to be sensitive to the spiritual world, and especially, to Him. God's primary way of communicating with us is for His Spirit to speak to our spirit through His Word.

Finally, we need to tune in, not only to tone and to temperature, but also to truth. When we worship "in spirit and in truth," we need biblical accuracy. Spiritual vitality doesn't come out of nowhere, and it doesn't come, as the Eastern religions suggest, by emptying our minds. Vibrant spiritual life develops when we fill our minds with God's truth and invite His Spirit to have His way with us. Paul made the connection between our minds and our wills in his letter to the Romans. For eleven chapters, he described the glorious grace of God. Then, at the beginning of chapter twelve, he began to describe how grace transforms our thinking, our desires, our relationships, and our choices. He wrote, "Therefore, I urge you, brothers, in view of God's mercy, to offer your bodies as living sacrifices, holy and pleasing to God—this is your spiritual act of worship. Do not conform any longer to the pattern of this world, but be transformed by the renewing of your mind. Then you will be able to test and approve what God's will is—his good, pleasing and perfect will" (Rom. 12:1–2). We simply cannot step into the full will of God without letting Him impart His Word to us through meditation, journaling, prayer, and obedience. That's how our minds are renewed. It's the only way.

Confirmation

Often—but not always—a word from God is confirmed by another person. I may have wanted to blow it off when the Spirit took me to Luke 22 to confront my pride, but when my mother called to say God had given her the same passage to share with me, I couldn't escape. I was nailed! God was beginning to take me on a difficult journey into the darkness of my own heart. He knew I'd looked for ways to explain away His message to me. Bad pizza? Working too hard? Was I looking at the wrong chapter in Luke? No, God didn't want me to have any questions about what He was saying, so He used someone I love and respect to confirm His word to me.

For months, I struggled. I grieved, and I was filled with anxiety. I thought I was going insane. Satan was, in fact, sifting me. I felt blown and thrashed like a bundle of wheat being bashed on the floor. It was one of the most agonizing times of my life. As I meditated on the passage, I realized that the process of sifting separates the valuable kernels of wheat from the chaff. This understanding gave me hope that God was doing something really good even though it felt really awful. Through it all, God reminded me over and over again of Jesus' implied promise to Peter in Luke 22:32: "But I have prayed for you . . . that your faith may not fail. And when you have turned back, strengthen your brothers." This assurance gave me hope that God wasn't finished with me in spite of how I felt. God gave me this word before I began wrestling with Him over my pride, and He gave it to me in two confirming, unmistakable ways: in my spirit and through my mother.

We can't base our lives on some vague hope of getting through hard times. We need a solid foundation of a word from God, often validated, repeated, and confirmed by someone we respect.

We can't base our lives on some vague hope of getting through hard times. We need a solid foundation of a word from God, often validated, repeated, and confirmed by someone we respect. Then, as we embrace the word and meditate on it, God breathes life into us with the refreshing wind of His Spirit.

We need to be careful whose voice we trust to confirm God's word. We shouldn't look for people who will tell us only what we want to hear. We need to look for those who have a proven track record of spiritual discernment, honesty, and encouragement. In many ways, those who deserve our trust have the same kind of tone and temperature as the Spirit. And when we hear them, we need to take it seriously. However, we also need to remember that everyone is fallible. People make mistakes. Even the most gifted and godly person sometimes misunderstands the whisper of God. As we grow, we'll learn to identify the people who have wisdom and enough courage to tell us the truth. Those people are worth their weight in gold. We may not like what they say, but they've earned a position of trust to say it to us.

Next Steps

The principles of getting and obeying a word from God apply to every believer, from the newest believer to old and seasoned pastors. God is a loving Father and a courageous King. He longs to share His heart with us, and He invites us to join Him in the dangerous, wild adventure of being His partner in building His kingdom and changing lives for eternity.

When I was frustrated with our church and sensed God had something more for us, I didn't know which way to turn. I uncovered a hundred different programs and read dozens of books. All the ideas sounded good, but none of them had the stamp of the Spirit for me. Then, God gave me a word from Matthew 6:33, and it all became clear. God wanted me to put His kingdom first by planting churches. Giving our church's finances away and sowing our people into a new church was the specific application of this Bible promise for me at that moment. The back part of this promise was for me as well: "and all these things will be added to you." As I pursued this word, God replaced frustration in my life with His favor and peace. I finally had clarity instead of confusion, peace and purpose instead of drifting from one good idea to another.

This promise from God, revealed in Scripture and illuminated by the Holy Spirit to my heart, became our rallying cry. We built upon the word, we obeyed what God asked us to do, and He showed up in major ways to "add all things to us." My obedience to the Holy Spirit's applied word has provided a roadmap for the adventure of a lifetime. As I walked that path, His word became the testimony of my life, and grace is the message of my entire church family.

When we don't have a word from Him, we're miserable (at least I am), but when we're sure God has spoken, we have new energy, direction, and courage to do things we've never done before.

Words from God, though, aren't just about churches and ministry. We need a word from God about our marriages, our children, our parents, our careers, our finances, our health, our hobbies, our habits, our past, our future, and everything else that matters. I believe God graciously gives us words if we earnestly seek Him and wait on Him to speak to us. When we don't have a word from Him, we're miserable (at least I am), but when we're sure God has spoken, we have new energy, direction, and courage to do things we've never done before. Of course, we're still human, and we still do dumb things. But the trajectory of our lives is different when we know we've heard from God. Setbacks are temporary instead of devastating, and we learn valuable lessons from our mistakes.

The King with His sleeves rolled up is also a King who speaks to His people. For years, we may have thought He was distant, indifferent, and inactive, but the shout of Scripture is that He's none of those things. He's present, He cares so much He still trembles with compassion for those He loves, and He's active—often visibly if we take time to notice, but also, always behind the scenes.

The Word of God is sitting on our shelves, waiting for us to open the book and let the Spirit impart it to our hearts. Like any relationship, our connection with God has ups and downs. At times, it seems like we can almost touch Him, but occasionally, it feels like He's visiting a different galaxy—and even worse, it may appear that He's showing up in others' lives but not ours . . . that's discouraging. We read, we meditate, we journal, we pray, and we obey all we know to obey, but God seems to have abandoned us. What in the world is going on?

There could be several reasons God is silent. God may have given us something to obey, but we've chosen not to. A principle of spiritual life is that God may not give us more directions until we've obeyed the commands He's already given us. We're saying, "God, speak to me," but He's saying, "I already did. When you obey what I've already told you, I'll be happy to give you more."

Another reason God may seem silent is that we're utterly exhausted. We can't even connect with our spouses, children, best friends, and dog. Why would we think we could have an intimate connection with an invisible God?

When we're burned out, we need rest. Like the prophet Elijah, we need to sleep a long time and get some good food. Even then, we may not bounce back quickly. We're not computers. We can't reboot at a moment's notice and be at full speed. We're complex mechanisms, and we need plenty of time and resources to recover.

Sometimes, God wants us to go deeper and spend more time with the word He has already given us. We want something fresh and new, but God isn't finished with the previous word. Many of us have short attention spans. We think we should always have the newest this or the latest that. God's purposes are far different than our culture's values. We shouldn't be surprised when He wants us to revisit past directives to forgive someone who has hurt us deeply, love someone who annoys us, and care for someone who can give us nothing in return. We always have more work to do in these areas.

God may take us through a time of darkness to test our faith to see if we'll keep trusting Him. Actually, this is God's purpose for us in all difficult times, but sometimes, it's especially dark and difficult, and we can't determine any cause at all. Author and professor, J. I. Packer assures us, "Sooner or later, God's guidance, which brings us out of the darkness into light, will also bring us out of light into darkness. It is part of the way of the cross."[15] All heroes of our faith were led into times of difficulty and darkness. Jesus faced forty days of temptation in the wilderness, friends' misunderstanding and religious leaders' condemnation, the cross, and the tomb. If we're going to follow Him, imitate Him, and be conformed to His image, we can expect at least a taste of the suffering He endured. Through all the pain, all the heroes of faith—especially Jesus—had a word from God. They persevered because God had given them a sense of hope that He was at work even when they couldn't see it.

In times of spiritual loneliness, we need to focus on the wonderful truths of God's love, grace, forgiveness, and power. Thank God, they're true whether we feel them or not. The silence of God should not be mistaken for the disapproval of God. It may mean that He knows we've grown enough to be tested—sometimes severely tested—by what seems to be His absence.

If we're not hearing from God, we need to diagnose the reason—without assuming the worst of us or of God. We may be very tired and need some rest. We may need to complete a task God has already given us. He may be testing us and taking us deeper in our faith. Or maybe, He's preparing other people and situations for the next word to us.

Just Do It

Too often, people leave church on Sunday and get up from their devotions each day without any sense that God has given them a mission. They feel entertained and maybe even inspired, but they don't have a clear idea of the next step they need to take. Real faith always takes action. James, the half-brother of Jesus, explained:

> Do not merely listen to the word, and so deceive yourselves. Do what it says. Anyone who listens to the word but does not do what it says is like a man who looks at his face in a mirror and, after looking at himself, goes away and immediately forgets what he looks like. But the man who looks intently into the perfect law that gives freedom, and continues to do

this, not forgetting what he has heard, but doing it—
he will be blessed in what he does (James 1:22–25).

> **We can study, learn, and meditate on all the wonderful truths of the Bible, but none of that will make a dent if we don't take steps to obey.**

We can study, learn, and meditate on all the wonderful truths of the Bible, but none of that will make a dent if we don't take steps to obey. After countless hours instructing His disciples, and more immediately, washing their feet as an example of selfless service, Jesus looked at them and said, "Now that you know these things, you will be blessed if you do them" (John 13:17). Obedience detonates God's blessings in our lives. It opens the floodgates of the Spirit's power to work in us and through us to change lives. Notice the nature of the obedience Jesus modeled. It wasn't preaching to thousands on a hillside, healing sick people, confronting self-righteous leaders, or raising the dead. Jesus took the role of the most humble house servant to wash the feet of the disciples. The primary way we obey Jesus is to be humble servants to those who are closest to us. When we prove ourselves in humility, gentleness, forgiveness, kindness, patience, and compassion, God will give us plenty of things to do.

Obeying God's Word brings all the power and purpose of the kingdom into our lives: our most important relationships, our finances, our careers, our friendships, and every other aspect of life.

Has God given you a word? Have you wrung every drop out of it so that it has become part of you? Are you obeying

Him in it? This is the way God's kingdom comes and His will is done on earth as it is in heaven.

Consider This

1. What are some ways we know God has given us a word we can count on and obey?

2. What is a word God has given you? Where are you in the process of embracing it and obeying it?

3. How does God use His written Word to melt our hearts with His love and strengthen our resolve to obey Him?

4. How would you define and describe meditation? What practices are most helpful to you as you let your mind and heart soak in God's truth? (Or what practices look like they might be helpful?) Explain your answer.

5. Describe the Holy Spirit's tone and temperature as He communicates with us.

6. Have you ever gone through an extended time of spiritual drought or darkness? Of the possible causes listed in this chapter, what might have been the cause in your case?

7. How have you seen obedience "detonate God's blessings" in your life?

8. What has God said to you as you have read this chapter?

chapter 8

Fully Alive

May God deliver us from self-righteous judging and make us, instead, merciful carriers of Christ's salvation and freedom everywhere we go.

Jim Cymbala

The people who enjoy the relationship with God described in this book don't live between the dusty covers of history books. The principles of putting God and His kingdom first, living by His Word, and watching Him explode blessings in our lives as we obey are *the normal Christian life!* We don't have to be Super Christians or desert monks to experience the intimacy, love, and power of a deep relationship with God. That's what He wants for all of us. I want to introduce you to a few people who are on this safari. Each of them faced difficulties and heartaches, but they trusted God. Each one is fully alive and aligned with the Spirit.

A Word from the Hospital Bed

Jana Snavely is the wife of Mark, one of the pastors on the staff at our church. A few years ago, she wasn't feeling well, so she went to the doctor. When the tests came back, the diagnosis was totally unexpected: leukemia. We were all devastated. Soon, she was really sick. She had been a beautiful person, inside and out, but as the disease took its toll, she lost weight, and her hair fell out in clumps.

For several months, we marshaled everyone to pray for Jana. Mark and their three children were heartbroken that she wasn't getting any better. As the disease progressed, it looked like she was going to lose the battle. One day, I visited her in the hospital. Mark stood behind me as I talked to her. He was crying. All their children were elementary age or younger. They were frightened and confused. Her skin was a sickly white, and the odor of death from her breath hung in the air.

As I stood by her bed, it seemed like only yesterday that Jana had lit up the room when she walked in. She and Mark had been part of a singing group at Oral Roberts University. Mark and Jana were beautiful people with beautiful voices. But Jana was anything but a straight, dull person. She had a wonderful—if quirky—sense of humor. One day, I was in my office talking on the phone, and she came in. I nodded to her and indicated the call wouldn't last much longer. She wasn't really interested in talking to me. At a costume store, she had bought a novelty piece that had a huge plastic derriere. As soon as I motioned to her that my call wouldn't take long, she turned around. I'm not sure what the other person on the phone was thinking as I laughed so hard, but I couldn't tell him what I'd seen! He'd never have believed it.

Now in the hospital bed, Jana looked like she might die any minute. Mark was heartbroken, and I had no answers. Her vibrant spirit was wasting away. She looked at me and asked, "Do you think this could have happened because I did something really bad in the past and God is punishing me?"

I shook my head, but the nagging thought wouldn't leave her. She continued, "I don't understand how this could have happened. I've been searching to figure out what I've done wrong to deserve this."

Jana's rapid deterioration shook us all. If this could happen to someone like Jana, it could happen to any of us.

While she lay in her hospital bed, and she slipped farther away each day, she wrote a song. In a time of supreme darkness, God gave her a ray of light. As she wrote the lyrics, God gave her a word from Jesus' assurance to Mary and Martha as their brother Lazarus lay cold in the tomb: "Just believe and you'll see the glory of God" (John 11:40 paraphrased). Jana began singing this song, again and again, each day. In this way, the word God gave her penetrated the depths of her heart and gave her hope. Gradually, her gnawing self-doubt and guilt were

> **Gradually, her gnawing self-doubt and guilt were replaced with renewed faith.**

replaced with renewed faith. (Listen to the song at www.facebook.com/janasnavelymusic) She wasn't sure what would happen to her—many people don't recover from the disease, no matter how many people pray—but she had a new sense of God's presence as she lay in her hospital bed.

The doctors tried new treatments for her disease. There were no guarantees. Jana was in and out of the hospital several times, vacillating between hope and heartache. But the disappointment she felt wasn't utter despair. She still had a strong foundation of confidence that God was near, kind, and active in her situation. Finally, God answered our prayers. Jana (and the rest of us who were praying) believed God and saw His glory in her healing. The treatment worked, and they officially declared her to be in remission.

Today, Mark and Jana serve at one of the churches we've planted. When we get together, we always talk about how God gave her strength to endure by giving her a word of hope. Jana would say the ordeal deepened her faith in God and her understanding of the pain others experience. To her, Mark and the kids are more precious than ever, and God has given her open doors to care for many hurting people. Before, she would have loved them and tried to help, but her journey of illness has dug a deep well of compassion that can only occur when a person has suffered deeply. Now, hurting people know Jana understands their fears and doubts, and that means everything to them.

New Direction

Brian Bolt grew up in a chaotic home. By the time he was thirteen, he had begun to use drugs to numb the pain and give him a buzz. A couple of years later, he ran away from home. Soon, he found his way from Maryland to the other side of the continent: California. He never really found a home. When he was old enough, he joined the Navy. During his time in the service, Brian found access to quantities of heroin. He went on countless binges, and his ability to think clearly was compromised. Eventually, he went AWOL, absent without leave.

While he was AWOL and living near the border with Mexico, Brian got involved in running drugs. He still had his Navy ID card, so he had easy access to border crossings. He went into Mexico, picked up a carload of drugs, drove into the United States, and unloaded it. He made an enormous amount of money, and he had all the trappings of a successful kingpin: cars, clothes, women, bling—the whole works.

When he was at the height of his operations, he got into a fight at a bar. A guy pulled out a pistol, put it up to Brian's head, and pulled the trigger. Before he passed out, he saw the pool of blood collecting on the floor. He thought, *I'm glad I'm dying because I have nothing to live for.*

The bullet ricocheted off the back of his skull and stopped next to his carotid artery, slowing the loss of blood. Brian remained barely conscious. A few minutes later, the ambulance arrived. On the way to the hospital, with the ambulance flying down the street with its siren blaring, the EMT realized Brian might not make it. He leaned down and asked, "Son, do you know Jesus?"

Brian mouthed the word, "No."

The EMT didn't miss a beat. He explained calmly, "You're probably going to die, so why don't we pray right now so you can trust in Christ."

The EMT prayed, and Brian gave his life to Jesus.

For the next 75 days, Brian was in and out of a coma. Because of the damage to his jaw, he couldn't swallow, so he couldn't eat or drink. Finally, Brian was well enough to be discharged from the hospital in San Diego. He had nowhere to go and no one to disciple him in his new faith, so he went back out on the streets. There, he met some people from a church called Victory Outreach. They assured him, "Brian, God has a plan for your life. You may have been an addict, but God has so much more for you. Why don't you come with us? We'll help."

They invited Brian to live in their recovery home, and there, God gave him a new vision for his life. He didn't learn techniques for staying sober. He found something better. Brian learned that God created him and rescued him for a purpose far bigger and more wonderful than any other purpose life can offer. Even if we've messed up really badly, God hasn't given up on us.

Brian learned that God created him and rescued him for a purpose far bigger and more wonderful than any other purpose life can offer.

Joining hands with God as His junior partner is Brian's motivation for sobriety, but even more, his drive is seeing God use him in the lives of addicts—men and women who have no hope apart from Christ. A kingdom vision has conquered Brian's craving for heroin, it's the cure for his emptiness, and it provides supportive, honest relationships that keep him strong. Yes, God miraculously saved him from a gunshot to the head, but the bigger miracle is his transformed life. God brought people around him who shared a kingdom perspective, and Brian ate it up. He realizes God has a plan for him that's far bigger than getting high, getting rich, or getting even.

From the beginning, the leaders at the recovery house threw Brian into the deep end of the pool. After he had been at the recovery house for a few weeks, they asked him to lead devotions the next morning. He told them he couldn't sing, and he didn't know any Bible verses. One of them said, "That's okay. You can lead us anyway."

Brian thought long and hard, and he realized he knew one song about Jesus. The next morning, he led them in that song. Then he led them again and again and again. When they sang it for the last time that morning, Brian realized, *God can use even me!*

A few weeks later, the leaders asked Brian to tell his story to the group. That seemed to go well. Not long after that day, they said, "Brian, we want you to preach at the next outdoor outreach we're going to have downtown." By this time, he realized God could use him in big ways. It may not have been the smoothest message ever presented, but the Spirit used it.

Brian looks back: "With every successive step I took, I gained confidence that I was no longer the hopeless addict I'd been. God had made me a new creation in Christ, and I had a purpose beyond my past."

Brian came to Pennsylvania to participate in The Master's Commission to be trained in ministry. Gerry, the leader of the training program, and I planned to have lunch one day. He brought Brian along. At lunch, Jerry and I caught up on our families, and then I turned to Brian and asked, "Tell me about yourself. What's your story?"

As he told his story, I wept with joy. Then I asked, "What do you think God wants you to do?"

Brian said, "I think God is leading me to start a church in the inner city of Pittsburgh."

My heart almost jumped out of my chest! I didn't stop to think, and I didn't wait to pray. I blurted out, "You're the guy I've been praying for!"

This is how God brought both sides of the story together: I'd been praying for decades for God to send me someone who could plant churches in the inner city. I had no idea who it would be, and I didn't imagine when I began praying that the person God would send was using and smuggling heroin into Southern California. As I prayed, God had His eye on Brian as he ran drugs across the border from Mexico.

A couple of months after our lunch together, Brian moved to Pittsburgh, and we helped him plant a church downtown. Today, City Reach Church is six years old. About 350 people worship there each week, and they've planted six other churches. Brian has a vision to plant a total of fifty churches in the most crime-infested, poverty-stricken areas of big cities. The primary audience includes prostitutes, drug addicts, and gang members, but ironically, these churches also attract wealthy people and young couples who live downtown. They love to see God at work in the lives of people who desperately need Him—which includes all of us.

From Death to Life . . . Two Ways

One of the people Brian's church reached is Lee Vozel. For many years, Lee's mother, Sandy, attended Allison Park Church. She always prayed for her sons, but one of them, Lee, was stuck in a life of drug addiction. When Brian planted the church and started a recovery home, Sandy saw it as potentially the answer to her prayers. She got all the information, talked to Lee, and asked him to go to the home. She was thrilled when he agreed to go, but when he arrived, it was clear that his only goal was to placate his mother. He had no intention of getting clean or giving his life to Christ. He brought drugs into the recovery home. After a few days, he overdosed on heroin. When others found him, he was lying dead on the floor in our men's recovery home.

When the emergency medical team arrived and assessed Lee's condition, he said, "He's gone. It's probably been twenty minutes, but I'm going to try one more thing." He injected a drug directly into his heart, and suddenly, Lee took a big breath. He was alive!

When Brian visited him in the hospital, Lee weakly said, "I think it's time for me to get right with God."

Brian made a call to California and worked it out for Lee to go to the same ministry where he had gotten clean years before. There, Lee found Christ, got off drugs, stayed off drugs, and discovered the burning purpose he saw in Brian. Eventually, he became the director of the men's home there. When Lee came back to Pittsburgh, he became the business director for the City Reach Church Network.

Sometimes, I almost laugh when I read particular passages of Scripture. In Ephesians, Paul said, "You were dead in your transgressions and sins . . . but . . . God . . . made us alive with Christ" (Eph. 2:1, 4). Lee Vozel was clinically dead, but God raised him and gave him new life—physically and spiritually.

Lee Vozel was clinically dead, but God raised him and gave him new life—physically and spiritually.

But don't forget the hidden part of this wonderful story. Sandy prayed for her son for over two decades. During that time, she didn't see much hope for Lee to become something God would use to touch others' lives, but she refused to give up on God. When Sandy started praying, God was already in motion, and He was in motion even when Sandy couldn't detect any movement at all. In the early years of her prayers, Lee was still lost and on drugs, and Brian, the eventual answer to her prayers, was still an addict and a drug runner out of Mexico.

Most of us think God needs to work in the way we con-
ceive of Him working, but God isn't bound by our ideas. He's
far more creative, and He has far more resources—and I think
God loves great stories even more than we do. God isn't "con-
strained to save by many or by few," by pure-hearted church
people or by proven programs. Sometimes, the answer to our
prayers comes from the most unlikely sources—flawed people
like Brian and Lee, and like you and me.

New Vision

My sister, Debbie, was diagnosed with diabetes when
she was only five years old. When she was in her twenties,
the disease began affecting her sight. Like Jana, Debbie sings
beautifully. At the time, she was traveling all over the world
with the Celebrant Singers. As I understand it, diabetics
have trouble with blood flow, so the body creates additional
blood vessels to compensate for the loss. When this happened in Debbie's eyes, it created inordinate pressure on the
retinas in both eyes, and they detached. She was going to be
blind. Her doctors performed surgery to reattach the retinas.
To minimize pressure during recovery, she had to lie on her
stomach in absolute darkness for several weeks.

Debbie had always been full of life, but those grueling
weeks threatened to crush her spirit. She was uncomfortable, she had to be waited on for her every need, she couldn't
minister to others and be with her friends in the group, and
her eyes hurt terribly. In her worst moments, she asked my
father, "Why is this happening to me? Where's God? I don't
know if I can stand this any longer!"

My dad patiently told her, "Debbie, don't waste this moment on bitterness. God is doing so much more than you

realize. He's at work. You can count on it. Don't come out of this with just the healing of your eyes. Go deeper. Come out of it with a message from God that you can give to the world."

With my father's encouragement, Debbie began to see her condition in a different way. Instead of eye surgery being a huge blockage to God's blessings, she realized it was a path to far more blessings than she could imagine. When the recovery time was over, Debbie was still blind in one eye, but she could see about 70 percent with the other one.

I vividly recall going to a church in Natrona Heights, Pennsylvania, to hear Debbie and her group sing. At one point, someone led her to a microphone at the front of the stage, and she told her story of trusting God in her darkest hour. Then she sang the lovely old hymn, "I Surrender All." The words declare, "All to Jesus I surrender, all to Him I freely give. I will ever love and trust Him, precious Jesus, Savior friend." And then the chorus burst forth: "I surrender all . . . all to thee my precious Savior, I surrender all." As I listened to Debbie sing, I'd never been so proud of her

Debbie's willingness to submit to God, no matter what, was—and is—beautiful.

in my life. There wasn't a dry eye in the place. Everybody was touched by Debbie's choice to surrender her eyesight and her life to God and live for something beyond her own healing. I was one of the people most deeply moved at that moment. Debbie's willingness to submit to God, no matter what, was—and is—beautiful. She shared her heart's prayer: "God, use even the problems with my eyes to advance your kingdom. Everything I am, everything I have, and everything

I will ever be is yours. In your love, wisdom, and strength, you can use every problem for your glory."

Normal

I preached a series of messages at our church using Scott Wilson's book, Act Normal. One Sunday, I spoke on the chapter about struggles in the Christian life being normal. In his book, Scott describes the apostle Paul's dedication to Jesus and the message of the gospel. We might think that God would have given such a treasured servant an easy time and made his way smooth. That's not what happened. In almost every city, Paul endured opposition, beatings, prison, and all kinds of suffering. When a prophet predicted he would be put in chains if he returned to Jerusalem, and his friends begged him to stay away, he boldly said, "I'm going no matter what happens. That's what God has called me to do, and I'm going to obey Him." In Jerusalem, he was almost killed by a mob before Roman soldiers saved him and put him in prison. He endured a series of trials and attempts on his life. When he couldn't get a fair hearing, he appealed to Caesar in Rome. Paul was going to have the opportunity to talk about the King of kings to the most powerful human ruler on earth. Then on the way to Rome, the ship encountered a fierce storm. Paul must have looked to heaven and asked, "Really, God, is this necessary? Does it have to be this hard?" When the captain and crew panicked, Paul, a prisoner, took command and brought everyone alive to shore. It was a miracle of faith and leadership. When the wet and exhausted men built a fire on the beach, a viper lunged out of the wood and bit Paul. Surely, people assumed, he was an evil man if a viper bit him. But Paul didn't die. After a long, incredible series of difficulties, Paul finally arrived in Rome—as a prisoner. Luke tells us Paul was under house arrest in Rome. He had endured a long ordeal to get there, and he was determined to make the most of it. Luke explained, "Boldly and without hindrance he preached the kingdom of God and taught about the Lord Jesus Christ" (Acts 28:31).

In my message, I explained that if we live with a God-given sense of purpose, the difficulties we experience take on new meaning. We don't see them only from a human point of view, so they aren't devastating. Paul knew that he had a destiny to take the gospel to Caesar in Rome. He knew angry crowds, shipwrecks, and prison couldn't stop the purpose of God from being fulfilled, so he saw the struggles as temporary impediments to God's greater purpose. He knew the snakebite couldn't stop him because God had a specific plan for his life. God gave Paul a vision for his life far beyond pleasure and comfort. The sailors and soldiers on the storm-tossed ship would never forget the faith of a prisoner who took over the ship and saved their lives. The people on the island where the snake bit Paul heard the gospel. Through it all, God had already been in motion.

A man from Rwanda attended our church for about fifteen years. When he was a little boy, Bosco and his family lived in Uganda, where both of his parents died of AIDS. His mother was a faithful Christian, but his father slept around, contracted the virus, and infected Bosco's mother. Just before his mother died, God gave her a promise from the Word that He would take care of her children. Being an orphan in a foreign land certainly didn't seem like an answer to his mother's prayers. Bosco bounced around from orphanage to orphanage. The boy was devastated by his mother's death. He attended church, but he walled God off from penetrating his heart.

After graduating from high school, Bosco earned a scholarship to study in the United States. He did well in college and graduated with a degree in business. He was in church the day I talked about pain and suffering being a normal part of the Christian life. Later, he told me, "It was like you and I were the only people in the room that morning. You were speaking directly to me." He heard me say, "Living on purpose makes living through difficulties less devastating," and the Spirit whispered to him, "Everything you've gone through in your life has a kingdom purpose. Don't miss it. Stop avoiding the pain that happened to you as a child. Do something *about* it so you and I can do something *with* it." At that moment, Bosco realized God was calling him to care for orphans of AIDS victims in Africa.

After the service, Bosco made a beeline to me. He told me God was directing him to start a nonprofit organization to care for mothers with HIV and their families in Uganda and Rwanda. He named it after his mother, The Mutete HIV/AIDS Foundation. The word God gave him is to use the pain of his past as a springboard to honor his mother's memory and care for these women and their children who are as lonely and hungry as he was. Bosco understands the intricacies of the problem far better than most. Part of the plan for the organization is to provide adequate food supplies for sick parents. Medication is available for the disease, but malnourished people can't properly assimilate the drugs. They need good food so the medicine will work. If more parents live, there will be fewer orphans.

When God gave Bosco a vision for how He could use the pain in a constructive way, he was willing to open his heart, experience God's healing, and let the heartaches of the past inspire compassionate action in the future.

Overflowing Comfort

A few years ago, I met with a small group of five men, including a man named Dave Herbert. We talked about God already being in motion and the fact that God doesn't waste our pain. We looked at Paul's perspective on his own suffering in his second letter to the Corinthians. Paul wrote that God "comforts us in all our troubles, so that we can comfort those in any trouble with the comfort we ourselves have received from God. For just as the sufferings of Christ flow over into our lives, so also through Christ our comfort overflows" (2 Cor. 1:4–5). After reading this passage, I asked, "What grace have you received that can overflow into others' lives?"

Dave said, "For years, I've been an alcoholic. I've gone to meetings, and God has turned my life around. Maybe God can use my experience to help other people who struggle with drugs and alcohol."

We did some investigating, and we found that Rick Warren's church was producing Celebrate Recovery, a Christian

When God gave Bosco a vision for how He could use the pain in a constructive way, he was willing to open his heart, experience God's healing, and let the heartaches of the past inspire compassionate action in the future.

version of the twelve steps of Alcoholics Anonymous. Dave and his wife, Cindy, flew to California to be trained, and when he returned, he led a ministry God has used to transform hundreds of lives. The spouses of addicts have their own set of difficulties because they try to control people who are out of control. Cindy began leading a group for the spouses of alcoholics and drug addicts. Like Bosco, Dave and Cindy realized God wanted to use their deepest pain and biggest struggles to help other people who are going through the same problems. Their call came from recognizing the abundant grace they had received from God, a grace that overflows into the lives of others.

An Unlikely Spokesman

Eric was a fourteen-year-old boy with a speech impediment. His disability left him feeling utterly miserable and alone. My son, Josh, befriended him at school and invited him to church. During a worship service, God spoke to him, "If you'll worship me, I'll set you free from your speech problem."

As Eric opened his mouth to praise God, something happened in his brain. He began to speak clearly and distinctly. People around him were amazed—no one was more amazed than Eric himself.

Today, years later, Eric has been trained in our ministry school and feels called to be a pastor. Sometimes, when I'm with him, I shake my head and say, "Eric, isn't it wonderful that God is using your lips and your voice to speak His gospel to people. You couldn't even talk before, but look at you now! Your life has become part of the message of hope and healing. Because of you, people know more of the love and miraculous power of God."

Every time Eric opens his mouth, he is reminded of the incredible grace of God, and his words carry not only the truth, but also the heart of God to those who hear him. It's a beautiful thing.

In Process

One of the myths of life is that if we can just get through the present, painful, awkward circumstance, we'll have it made. When this is over, we're sure life will be far better. This may feel like hope, but it's hope in the wrong thing: the empty promise of an easy life. Life is filled with a mixed bag of joys and disappointments, hopes and fears, successes and failures. When we attach our hopes to a change of circumstances, we may feel relieved for a short while, but we're soon deeply disappointed to find ourselves in the next difficulty. "It's not fair!" we may say to God, to ourselves, or to anyone who'll listen.

If we attach our hope to a person—the only One who is perfectly loving, wise, and strong—we'll be grateful for all the blessings, and we can have confidence even in the middle of darkness and difficulties. Jesus is always more than enough.

If we attach our hope to a person—the only One who is perfectly loving, wise, and strong—we'll be grateful for all the blessings, and we can have confidence even in the middle of darkness and difficulties. Jesus is always more than enough.

Don't get attached to the false hopes of faultless children, a perfect spouse, plenty of money, a big promotion, and a pain-free life. Don't trust in your ability to make life work and control circumstances by following rules. Let the wonder of grace and the mystery of a wild, good God fill your heart. Don't put Him in a box. Let Him out, and invite Him to have His way with you. If you're willing, He'll take you on adventures full of risks, setbacks, and marvelous escapes. You won't be on your own. Jesus will be your guide, your hero, and your best friend.

Without this sense of adventure, life can get extremely boring, and we can become self-absorbed. We spend our time and resources on the tiny dot of our pleasure, our prestige, and our possessions. God offers us far more than that! Every great movie and stirring novel is full of seemingly insurmountable difficulties and brave heroes. If we want a life absent of conflict, our stories will be pathetically dull. I'm not suggesting that you create difficulties. Not at all. But when we put our hand in Jesus' hand and follow Him, He communicates the tenderness of His heart, and He shares with us the pain of a broken world. It's both, not one without the other.

Some people may come to the end of this book and think, *Yeah, I understand what you're saying, but I'm still not sure I'm all in.* Fair enough. Faith is a gift from God, and the desire to obey is a gift, too. Some would respond, "But don't we have to make a choice to trust in God and obey Him?" Yes, trusting God is both a gift and a choice. In both, the Holy Spirit is at work in us—that's part of the mystery of a life of faith. The Scriptures invite us to "look to Jesus" and let the Spirit melt, mold, and inspire our hearts to follow Him wherever He leads. A pastor told me he had talked to a friend who was struggling with obeying God. The pastor asked his friend, "Do you want to obey Him?"

His friend thought for a few seconds and said, "To be honest, I'm not sure."

The pastor then asked, "Do you want to want to obey Him?"

The friend looked surprised by the question and then replied, "Yes, that's where I am. I want to want to."

"Then start there," the pastor suggested, "and see what God does in your heart."

We can start wherever we are. If our hearts aren't filled with wonder, we can be honest with God. If we don't want to love and obey God, we can tell Him the truth—He already knows anyway. Our beginning point might be to want to want Him. That desire, too, is a gift from God. He'll use even this toehold to begin something wonderful in our lives.

Our responses to life's ups and downs tell us a lot about the condition of our hearts. Many of us need to evaluate our expectations. If we get disproportionately upset about relatively little problems, our hopes and expectations are out of balance. (If you're not sure about yours, ask your spouse or your best friend.) God is already in motion. He's preparing breakthrough moments for us. If we'll look for Him and follow His lead, we'll step into those holy moments. They aren't simple, pure, and clean. They are far more often like Paul's tenacious commitment to take the gospel back to Jerusalem and then to Rome—a story full of twists and turns, setbacks and glories, evil people and trusted friends. In the middle of our stories, we may lose sight of God, but we can

> **God is already in motion. He's preparing breakthrough moments for us. If we'll look for Him and follow His lead, we'll step into those holy moments.**

be sure that He's always present, He cares deeply, and He's still active behind the scenes. Sooner or later, He'll show Himself and speak His Word to us. We can count on it. If we find the courage to trust Him, we'll step into something amazing—not perfect, not easy, but more fulfilling than we have ever imagined. God delights in redeeming the past— all of our sins and wounds—and creating something new and beautiful out of them. That's what makes great stories. Those are the kinds of life dramas we want to tell our children and grandchildren.

If you haven't started creating those stories, start now. If you're in the middle of them, keep it up. God is smiling with every step you take.

Consider This

1. Which of the stories in this chapter connected with your life and your heart? Explain your answer.

2. What grace have you received that can overflow into others' lives?

3. How might God use your past—sins and wounds—to give
    you compassion for others who struggle with the same
    kinds of difficulties? Is there a ministry you can plug
    into? Is God calling you to start something new?

4. What are some false hopes that distort our expectations
    and create disappointments? What are some false hopes
    in your life that have surfaced as you've read this book?
    What does God want you to do about them?

5. What are the two or three most important principles
    or truths you've learned from this book? How have they
    already reshaped your relationship with Jesus? How do
    you expect them to continue to impact your life?

6. Take some time to think, pray, and complete the Dis-
    cernment Map on the following pages.

Discernment Map

The book has identified a number of important principles about finding and following the will of God. This exercise is designed to pull them together into a cohesive whole.

Find an extended period of time (or several blocks of time) when you aren't rushed or distracted. Ask God to give you His heart and wisdom as you consider your response to these questions. Some of your answers may be instantly clear, but the answers unfold over time for most of us—so be patient and persistent as you pursue God's heart and His purpose for your life.

1. Think over the timeline of your life. What are the times and circumstances when you experienced wounds, crushing disappointment, betrayal, loss, a prodigal life-style, failure, or other sources of heartache?

2. Has God already used one or more of those experiences to give you compassion for those who are going through similar struggles? If so, describe the ways God has used you.

3. How might God use wounds and sins that have remained buried to bring a new wave of healing and create new sources of compassion for others?

4. Take time to pray, "God, thank you that you have chosen to love and forgive me by your grace. I now choose to forgive myself. I release myself to step into the future you have for me."

5. As you've prayed, read, and thought, how would you answer the question, "What's God's problem?" What is a problem in your community or the world that burdens your heart?

6. If God is already in motion, how do you see Him at work in your life and around you?

7. Have you received a word from God about a problem or burden? What passages of Scripture has He given you to guide and motivate you to meet this need?

8. Who is a trusted friend or mentor who has confirmed the word God has spoken to you? (Or who might be that person?)

9. What does it mean for you to put Christ and His kingdom first in your life? What are God's promises to you? What are the risks and challenges?

10. All of us (at least those who are honest) have some reluctance to be "all in" with Jesus. What are your fears and doubts? How does the word God has given help you stay focused and persistent?

11. What is your next right step? How and when will you take it? What can you expect to happen?

12. What kinds of stories do you want to tell your children? Are you actively and courageously creating those stories today? If not, what do you need to change?

Endnotes

1 St. Augustine, *Confessions*, 397, I, 1.

2 Quote cited on Quoteland.com, www.quoteland.com/topic/Basketball Quotes/212/

3 Adapted from Henry Blackaby and Claude King, *Experiencing God* (Nashville: B&H Books, 2008).

4 Cited by Jason E. Hill in *More than Words: Moving Beyond Lip-Service Christianity to True Faith* (Nashville: WestBow Press, 2011), 111.

5 Bruce Wilkinson, *You Were Born for This* (Colorado Springs: Multnomah Books, 2009), 107f.

6 Cited by Clyde S. Kilby in *The Christian World of C. S. Lewis* (Grand Rapids: Wm. B. Eerdmans Publishing Company, 1995), 68.

7 Cited by Richard Stearns, *The Hole in Our Gospel* (Nashville: Thomas Nelson, 2009), 9.

8 J. I. Packer, *Knowing God* (Downers Grove: InterVarsity Press, 1973), 196.

9 Jonathan Edwards, "The Christian Pilgrim," *The Works of Jonathan Edwards*, vol. 2 (Carlisle, PA: Banner of Truth Trust, 1974), 244.

10 A. W. Tozer, *The Pursuit of God* (Colorado Springs, CO: World Literature Crusade, 2009), 13.

11 N. T. Wright, *Following Jesus* (Grand Rapids, MI: Eerdman's Publishing Company, 1994), 113.

12 John White, *The Fight* (Downers Grove, IL: InterVarsity Press, 1976), 16.

13 I've used the New International Version and The Message in this book. Other popular versions are the English Standard Version and the New Living Translation.

14 Wayne Cordiero, *Divine Mentor* (Bloomington, MN: Bethany House Publishers, 2008), 101f.

15 J. I. Packer, *Knowing God Through the Year* (Downers Grove: InterVarsity Press, 2004), 283.

About the Author

Jeff Leake is a graduate of Central Bible College with a BA in Bible, and he graduated from the Assemblies of God Theological Seminary with an MA in Missiology. These themes—biblical and missional—are evident in his writing and his leadership as the Lead Pastor of Allison Park Church, located in the north hills of Pittsburgh, Pennsylvania.

During Jeff's twenty-one years as Lead Pastor, he has founded many organizations. Reach Northeast is a church planting network designed to facilitate new churches throughout the northeast United States. The Network of Hope is a non-profit organization designed to work through local churches to bring lasting change through very practical forms of community ministry. The Northeast Ministry School was established to train church planters, missionaries, and members of church planting teams. Jeff currently serves as the president of Reach Northeast and the Northeast Ministry School, and he is the Vice President of the Network of Hope.

Jeff and his wife, Melodie, have five children. Melodie serves on the staff at Allison Park Church as the pastor over the Women's Ministry. Jeff and Melodie have spoken at leadership conferences in Sweden, Nicaragua, Tanzania, Rwanda, India, and in many regional leadership events throughout the United States. The themes of "God in Motion" are a major part of the subject matter for these conferences and events.

Using *God in Motion* in Groups and Classes

This book is designed for individual study, small groups, and classes. The best way to absorb and apply these principles is for each person to individually study and answer the questions at the end of each chapter then to discuss them in either a class or a group environment.

Each chapter's questions are designed to promote reflection, application, and discussion. Order enough copies of the book for everyone to have a copy. For couples, encourage each to have their own book so they can record their individual reflections.

A recommended schedule for a small group or class might be:

Week 1

Introduce the material. As a group leader, tell your story, share your hopes for the group, and provide books for each person. Encourage people to read the assigned chapter each week and answer the questions.

Weeks 2–9

Each week, introduce the topic for the week and share a story of how God has used the principles in your life. In small groups, lead people through a discussion of the questions at the end of the chapter. In classes, teach the principles in each chapter, use personal illustrations, and invite discussion.

Personalize Each Lesson

Don't feel pressured to cover every question in your group discussions. Pick out three or four that had the biggest impact on you, and focus on those, or ask people in the group to share their responses to the questions that meant the most to them that week.

Make sure you personalize the principles and applications. At least once in each group meeting, add your own story to illustrate a particular point.

Make the Scriptures come alive. Far too often, we read the Bible like it's a phone book, with little or no emotion. Paint a vivid picture for people. Provide insights about the context of people's encounters with God, and help people in your class or group sense the emotions of specific people in each scene.

Focus on Application

Encourage group members to be authentic. This and the questions at the end of each chapter will help your group take big steps to apply the principles they're learning. Share how you are applying the principles in particular chapters each week, and encourage them to take steps of growth, too.

Three Types of Questions

If you have led groups for a few years, you already understand the importance of using open questions to stimulate discussion. Three types of questions are *limiting, leading,* and *open.* Many of the questions at the end of each day's lesson are open questions.

Limiting questions focus on an obvious answer, such as, "What does Jesus call himself in John 10:11?" These don't stimulate reflection or discussion. If you want to use questions like this, follow them with thought-provoking, open questions.

Leading questions require the listener to guess what the leader has in mind, such as, "Why did Jesus use the metaphor of a shepherd in John 10?" (He was probably alluding to a passage in Ezekiel, but many people don't know that.) The teacher who asks a leading question has a definite answer in mind. Instead of asking this kind of question, you should just teach the point and perhaps ask an open question about the point you have made.

Open questions usually don't have right or wrong answers. They stimulate thinking, and they are far less threatening because the person answering doesn't risk ridicule for being wrong. These questions often begin with "Why do you think . . . ?" or "What are some reasons that . . . ?" or "How would you have felt in that situation?"

Preparation

As you prepare to teach this material in a group or class, consider these steps:

Carefully and thoughtfully read the book. Make notes, highlight key sections, quotes, or stories, and complete the reflection section at the end of each day's chapter. This will familiarize you with the entire scope of the content.

As you prepare for each week's class or group, read the corresponding chapter again and make additional notes.

Tailor the amount of content to the time allotted. You won't have time to cover all the questions, so pick the ones that are most pertinent.

Add your own stories to personalize the message and add impact.

Before and during your preparation, ask God to give you wisdom, clarity, and power. Trust Him to use your group to change people's lives.

Most people will get far more out of the group if they read the chapter and complete the reflection each week. Order books before the group or class begins or after the first week.

To Order More Copies

To order more copies of this book,
go to www.influenceresources.com